IQ plus EQ

The Arrow and the Hoisting Crane

Feliciano T Bantilan, Jr

Limit of Liability/Disclaimer of Warranty:

Dedication

To my three sons:
Hans, Kurt, and Niels;

To the young ones like them;

Investing a little sum now, holding it till your retirement will grow to take care of you in your golden years.

Table of Contents

PREFACE.. 6

PLAN OF BOOK 8

ACKNOWLEDGMENT 11

INTRODUCTION: IQ VERSUS EQ 12

PART 1: EQ—WEAKNESSES OF HUMAN NATURE 18

    CHAPTER 1: SHORT TIME HORIZON.................................20
    CHAPTER 2: POOR INTUITIVE STATISTICIAN.....................26
    CHAPTER 3: LOSS AVERSION 37
    CHAPTER 4: ENVY AND HERD MENTALITY 42
    CHAPTER 5: FEAR AND GREED 46

PART 2: IQ—UNDERSTANDING STOCK INVESTING 49

    CHAPTER 6: NATURE OF PORTFOLIO RETURNS................51
    CHAPTER 7: DIFFICULTY IN VALUING A BUSINESS.............71
    CHAPTER 8: THE WORLD OF MUTUAL FUNDS 80
    CHAPTER 9: GREENBLATT INVESTING APPROACH 90

PART 3: IQ IN SUPPORT OF EQ—AN INVESTING APPROACH 101

    CHAPTER 10: THE ARROW AND THE HOISTING CRANE.............103
    CHAPTER 11: WHICH INVESTING APPROACH?....................112
    CHAPTER 12: RE-PROGRAMMING OUR MIND 119
    CHAPTER 13: MANAGING OUR PORTFOLIO 127

CONCLUSION: IQ AND EQ 134

APPENDIX: QUESTIONS MY SON ASKED 142

ABOUT THE AUTHOR...151

    OTHER BOOKS BY THE AUTHOR 153

Preface

I first came to stock investing partly out of curiosity; and partly out of the possibility of making my money work hard for me, while I attend to other things. When I had to leave the usual workplace due to my Parkinson's illness, suddenly the possibility of my money working hard for me became a necessity as I no longer could work for money.

Since then, there has been no turning back. Investing is one of the twin blades I now wield to cut through life – the other is writing poetry and prose, given my limitations. I have to earn my keep, especially with my illness requiring many supplements. Indeed, my money working hard for me started out as a mere possibility, metamorphosed into a necessity; and finally became a reality, amply providing me for my needs as a Parkinson's patient.

This book grew out of a series of essays I wrote for my children—my three sons. My aim was to educate them about investing in the stock market. My ultimate goal was to have each open an account with a broker and start investing in the stock market—hoping that they will take to stock investing as a lifetime activity.

Of my three sons, one, uninterested in picking stocks, opted to open an account in a mutual fund managed by Greenblatt and his associates. The other two prefer to pick stocks and opened their accounts accordingly.

My sons are young. They have a long time horizon ahead of them—ideal for stock investing—40, 50 years or more. They have recently graduated from college and are working in their respective fields. I stressed to them that while they are young to regularly set aside money they do not need for their daily expenses—money they can set aside for years until they retire. Instead of putting the said regular small amount of money in a bank account, they should put it instead in a mutual fund account or a stock brokerage account.

Like any parent, I want my sons to live a comfortable life in their golden years, when healthcare is paramount, where extra funds will go a long way to ease suffering. And being in the midst of experiencing it, I want them to be ready for the vicissitudes attendant in advancing years. I would not have managed my illness as well as I have, if not for the latest advances in molecular biology. Unfortunately, this happy circumstance is only possible if one is able to pay. The molecular mechanisms of my illness would have gone unaddressed, and I would have been unimaginably worse off than I am now.

My aim in re-working out the essays into a book format for a wider readership is no different from my original aim: to educate the young and those who are interested on how to invest in the stock market.

My advice is based on hard-earned knowledge, coming from my experience as an investor in the stock market for over 17 years. Starting from ignorance, I navigated through the confusing and confused world of stock market investing. I read the works of the great masters—Benjamin Graham, Philip Fisher, Warren Buffett (his essays), Joel Greenblatt, Ken Fisher, and others. I read on developments in behavioral economics, in particular in behavioral finance.

I came to stock investing with the aim of reaching rock bottom—to dig deeply to arrive at what I call the "ultimate" principles of sound investing in the stock market. I am satisfied to have found the "perennial principles" as enunciated by the great masters, with their modern implementation for the small investor by the approach developed by Joel Greenblatt.

My hard-earned knowledge I shared with my three sons, I am proud to share with you.

Plan of Book

This book, "IQ plus EQ: The Arrow and the Hoisting Crane", opens with an *Introduction* giving an overview of the roles of IQ and EQ in stock investing. It stresses this point: *our EQ has the lead role in all our decisions, including investing decisions.*

The book has three parts:

Part 1, *EQ—Weaknesses of Human Nature,* deals with issues on human nature that tend to make us lousy investors. We will detail the traits in our nature that detract from our goal of making money in the stock market.

We start in chapter 1 with a key problem: the fact that we have a short time horizon compared to the stock return time horizon. The mismatch of the two is a source of problems to many investors. In chapter 2, we will discuss an important characteristic of the human mind—our weakness in statistical reasoning. We have no intuitive grasp of random events, as we have of causal events.

Then, we move on to the behavior of loss aversion in chapter 3: we feel pain looking at our portfolio when it is "dripping" in red, prompting us to actions detrimental to our goal of making money. Envy and herd mentality are the subject in chapter 4. We are naturally envious when others have higher returns and are likely to imitate what they do with their portfolio. Finally, in chapter 5, we tackle the twin emotions of fear and greed that could send the stock market crashing down.

Part 2, *IQ—Understanding Stock Investing,* presents the minimum set of notions on how the stock market works. We start by dissecting the nature of portfolio returns in chapter 6. Then, we explain in chapter 7 the difficulty in valuing a business. Valuing a business is central to investing in the stock market. We will find out that we can circumvent the actual valuation by what I call the Greenblatt method. We move on to the world of mutual funds in chapter 8. And in chapter 9, we present Greenblatt's approach to investing; and arguments why the value-weighted index performs best among various indexes.

Part 3, *IQ in support of EQ—An Investing Approach,* tackles the choice of an investing approach, in the process addressing the distinct roles of Reason and Emotion—of IQ and EQ. We open Part 3 with a presentation of a two-component model of stock portfolio return—*the arrow and the hoisting crane*—in chapter 10. Stripped to its bottom line, investing in the stock market all boils down to: *portfolio return.*

Then, we move on to answer the question which approach do we choose to invest in stocks in chapter 11. Having chosen an approach, we go to the issue of re-programming our mind to better execute the chosen approach as an investor in chapter 12. Finally, in chapter 13, we talk about the needed housekeeping to maintain our portfolio.

In view of our difficulty in dealing with our emotions, the question we pose is: can we reduce investing to a step-by-step procedure so that emotions, if we so choose, do not play a role at all? The approach—the Greenblatt approach—that I recommend can be broken down to specific steps that can be mechanically executed, where emotions do not play a role, if you follow the guidelines.

But, for all the "mechanicalness" of the approach, where emotions are absent, a moronic EQ can still pull the plug, so to speak. Going all the way, I believe this approach—the Greenblatt approach—is ideal for a small investor. I use it myself.

The book concludes by revisiting the issue of IQ and EQ, now with a grasp of our "biases", as well as a grip on the two-component dynamics of stock returns—*the arrow and the hoisting crane.*

I have added as an appendix the questions my son asked me for further clarifications on points in the essays I sent to my three sons. The text is exactly as the original—both my son's questions and my answers—except for a few corrections in punctuations and references. The questions are penetrating and earnest. My answers too are earnest, as well as, I believe correct.

Acknowledgment

I am grateful to the following authors for their expositions on various aspects of the financial markets. This book would not be possible without their writings. The number in parenthesis is the number of books I read by the same author(s): Lawrence A. Cunningham (1), Benjamin Graham (1), Benjamin Graham and David Dodd (1), Phillip Fisher (1), Joel Greenblatt (3), Ken Fisher (5), Jim Cramer (3), Daniel Kahneman (1), Robert Hagstrom (2), John Neff (1), Phil Town (2), Clark Winter (1), Jeremy Siegel (2), Pat Dorsey (2), Robert Kiyosaki et al (5), Timothy Vick (1), John Burr Williams (1), Peter Bernstein (1), James O'Loughlin (1).

Despite her busy schedule, my wife, Cynthia Bantilan still managed to contribute to making this a better book—like the change in the subtitle; the book cover. I deeply appreciate her love and support.

I appreciate the incisive and encouraging comments from my sister, Sr. Librada Bantilan, MIC.

My thanks go to my three sons—Kurt, Niels, and Hans—for their suggestions on the book cover; to Kurt, for his helpful and insightful comments on the overall organization of the book; to Niels, for his perceptive questions and suggestions.

I am especially grateful to Prof Joel Greenblatt for providing a method together with a free website for small investors like me, enabling me to cease pretending to do valuations of businesses. If one understands his method, then one sees his combined ranking of earnings yield and return on invested capital is equivalent to valuing businesses. One attains the same result—I may add more systematically—of "paying a lot less" without explicitly valuing any business.

Introduction: IQ versus EQ

"I can calculate the motion of heavenly bodies but not the madness of people".
Sir Isaac Newton

Newton's loss of 20,000 pounds (2.72 million in 2009 US dollars) invested in the South Sea Company in the bubble in the 1720's was the occasion of the quote above. The quote, as well as the recent market crash in 2007-2009, should serve as a call to heed the findings of modern cognitive psychology.

We are not what we think we are

Over the millennia, people's behavior derives from the same human nature. Between the bubble in the 1720's and the market crash in 2007-2009, is shared the same psychological dynamics. The difference between the two times is the significant advance in our knowledge of human nature.

Both debacles call our attention to the experimental findings of modern cognitive psychology in the last 20 years or so—*that we humans are not what we think we are. Experiments show that we behave as if two systems are operating in our minds, labeled System 1 and System 2 by Daniel Kahneman, a co-winner of the 2002 Nobel Prize in Economics. System 1 is thinking—fast, automatic, effortless and **emotional**. System 2 is thinking—slow, deliberate, effortful and **logical**. Moreover, System 1 plays the **lead** role, while System 2 plays the **support** role. Furthermore, System 1 "biases" may lead us to make decision mistakes.*

What the findings summarized above tell me is that we humans are *not rational—error-free*; but, *emotional—error-prone, open to corrections with the use of our reason.*

Here is the link between the pitfalls in *stock market investing* and the findings of *modern psychology:* our Emotion, open to modulations by our Reason, orchestrates our investing decisions; due to "biases", our Emotion is prone to errors in judgment.

In a crowd of investors, such errors in judgment could spread like a wildfire producing what Newton decried as the "madness of people".

For the purposes of this book, I call System 1—EQ—the emotion quotient or emotional intelligence. And I call System 2—IQ—the intelligence quotient.

IQ and EQ defined

IQ refers to *intelligence* as commonly understood. EQ refers to *emotion quotient,* or, *emotional intelligence.* When someone presents you a math puzzle to solve, certain mental operations are set into motion in your brain. The capacity for solving such type of puzzles—we call IQ or intelligence.

An analogous case in stock market investing is to understand the rationale of an investing approach. Even here, EQ is involved in deciding whether to exert the effort to understand the material or not. IQ is involved in the process of understanding the material itself.

When an unexpected loud knock at the entrance door of your house at half past midnight confronts you, the puzzle on what to do sets into motion different mental operations, with some overlap with operations in the previous example. The capacity for solving such type of puzzles we call EQ or emotional intelligence.

An analogous instance in stock market investing is what to do, say, when your portfolio return drops 15% in a day. Here, your EQ may short-circuit the input from your IQ of its understanding of the situation; instead, act immediately based on prior knowledge in a package we call instinct, as our ancestors were prone to do in the savannahs in Africa. In the grip of fear the decline will continue, thereby losing more of your hard-earned money, you decide to quickly run away from the stock market by dumping all shares immediately, as fast as you can.

It is clear from the two examples above the *lead* role of System 1 or EQ in decision-making. An indication of the role of our emotion in decision-making unexpectedly arose from the case of a man who lost the emotional centers in his brain in an accident. The logical centers, though, were intact. The man's decision-making would be that much easier now with "noise" eliminated, so the researchers thought. They were in for a big surprise! The opposite was just the case. The man could not decide when given options. He was just indifferent.

Educating our emotions

We decide on the basis of online information or stored knowledge. Online information is information we acquire as we decide. Stored knowledge is either our past experience or an inherited tendency. A way to overcome a tendency is to acquire new information from which our emotions can draw upon in making decisions. This is what I call educating our emotions.

Say, your portfolio return drops by 5% from yesterday. Being loss averse, you are anxious what to do. Your gut feels something "serious" is causing the drop. However, if you learn returns naturally fluctuate in value, then your emotions have a new basis to draw upon for action. With this new knowledge, your emotions could shift from anxiety to cautious "serenity". This is what I mean by educating our emotions.

Behavioral Economics

Human behavior is the province of psychology. In the past, psychology did not usually figure in discussions on finance, in particular on investing. The behavior assumed in economics or finance is that of a human as a rational animal, dubbed *Homo economicus*. To be rational is defined as internal consistency in making decisions, with the rider that decision-making is free from mistakes. This notion of humans, called *Econs* in the book *Nudge* by Richard Thaler and Cass Sunstein, regarded as the bible of behavioral economics, implies an infinite capacity of mind to follow rules of logic error-free.

However, the pioneering work of Daniel Kahneman and Amos Tversky introduced a new, wholly different perspective on humans—the real, not the idealized kind—subsequently, giving birth to behavioral economics. The work won the Nobel Prize for economics in 2002. Real humans are not rational, in the sense defined above; or what is referred to as the Milton Friedman sense, or the Chicago School sense.

Real humans—called *Humans* in the same book *Nudge*—are only reasonable, and subject to innate weaknesses or biases that open them to make mistakes. They may act not consistent with their self-interest.

Here is another way of putting it: to repeat, *we humans are not rational—error-free; but, emotional—error-prone, open to corrections with the use of our reason.*

All of us believe we are rational. It is others who are emotional. We behave as if we are rational—only to find out we are far from being rational, especially in times of stress.

There is no clearer demonstration of our spectacular lack of rationality, than what is shown in mass sell-offs during bear markets.

Addressing our EQ: actual human nature

This book argues that to make better investing decisions in the stock market, we have to understand the workings of human nature. To make money in the stock market, we have to avoid contracting what I call the Newtonian "madness" in all its manifestations—big and small.

One may have the requisite IQ; but, not the requisite EQ.

The book starts from the assumption of behavioral economics that real humans, *Humans* in contrast to *Econs,* do not act with Friedman rationality error-free; but, with Kahneman reasonableness error-prone. It rejects the idealized humans.

It was natural for economics or finance not to use psychology in its considerations on decision making. Whatever trait was needed was already encompassed by the single trait of perfect rationality, supplemented with infinite capacity to process information.

However, as Kahneman and Tversky amply demonstrated the human mind is not what we assumed it to be. It has a built-in, systematic way of responding to the external world—what they call its "biases" that could lead us to mistakes, including catastrophic ones.

These mistakes would not have occurred if we were perfectly rational. Bubbles and crashes—and yes the "madness of people" do not occur if we are perfectly rational.

We are *Humans,* though, and not *Econs.*

And this brings us squarely to the need of understanding real humans: their actual nature.

Framing the whole discussion

To frame the whole discussion in this book, I summarize a successful approach to stock market investing in two simple statements: (1) know human nature; and (2) know the nature of stock returns.

We will explore the nature of stock returns in Part 2 and 3. We will introduce a novel way of coming to grips with stock returns by the metaphor of *the arrow and the hoisting crane.*

What is human nature? Where does it come from? How is human nature a hindrance to successful stock market investing? To explore these questions, we now move on to Part 1.

Part 1: EQ—Weaknesses of Human Nature

"Individuals who cannot master their emotions are ill-suited to profit from the investment process."

Benjamin Graham

The legacy of Daniel Kahneman and Amos Tversky is their pioneering experimental study on "biases" inherent in human nature. Knowing the "biases" enables us to understand our behavior and those of others in our day-to-day living. They are equally applicable in understanding our behavior in the stock market. This is the whole thrust of Part 1 of this book.

Understanding human nature enables us to see opportunities opened up by other people; at the same time it enables us, with great difficulty, to restrain our emotions. The madness of people refers to actions people take prodded by their emotions, possibly resulting in a permanent loss of investment capital.

We will discuss in detail the component traits of human nature that together lead to a self-defeating behavior in the stock market—in a word, to madness.

The origin of human nature

Some seven million years ago, a common ancestor, which probably looked more like a chimp than a human, gave rise to two lines of ancestry—that of humans, and that of chimps. It took that much time to sculpt a chimp-like creature to the upright-walking, tool-making *Homo sapiens*.

Technologies used in the Human Genome Project, enable us to sequence the genomes of humans and chimps. And we find that 98.4% of our genome is identical with that of the chimp. The 1.6% difference makes a huge difference. It must involve key genes that make possible our language ability, our highly developed consciousness, etc.

We can understand our behavior today only in terms of our evolutionary history. Eons of time in the evolutionary "Garden of Eden", in the savannahs in Africa, sculpted the body and mind of ancestors in our lineage. The result was human nature. And it is the same human nature that we inherit animating our behavior today.

Preview

In the following five chapters, we will discuss our weaknesses—the biases in the way our mind operates—that predispose us to what Newton decried the "madness of people". It is exactly like our predisposition to fear of snakes.

Chapter 1: Short Time Horizon

"The investor's chief problem - and even his worst enemy - is likely to be himself."

Benjamin Graham

We begin in this chapter an extended inward exploration of our mind, the automatic ways we respond to the promptings of the external world, focusing on those relevant to stock market investing decisions.

We explore the serious implications of the fact our psychological time horizon is short. It is an in-born trait, just like our fear of spiders. Due to this trait, we tend to err in our decisions involving time expectations. Such decisions could result in a permanent loss of investment capital.

1.1 Incommensurate time horizons

Incommensurability seems to be a feature of our notions and perceptions about the external world. Since the early Greeks, we found the incommensurability between the side of a square and its diagonal, for example. No matter how we slice and dice a side of a square, we cannot express the ratio of the diagonal to a side as a ratio of whole numbers.

Psychologically, we find ourselves in an analogous situation with respect to two time periods important in stock investing: our psychological time horizon and the stock-return assessment time period. The two are incommensurate.

Our time expectations for results are short, indeed. We want the results now. The longer the time, the more impatient we become. Short-time horizon, however, is a characteristic disposition we have in our dealings with anything. As indicated above, our sense of time horizon is an inherited trait from our ancestors in the savannahs in Africa.

Then, as now, the alternation of night and day, the rise and set of sun fix the rhythm of our lives. This time period nicely wraps the daily activities of our ancestors then, as well as our daily activities now. Unhappily, the time the Earth takes to rotate about its axis does not happen to jibe with an important time period—the stock-return assessment time period.

1.2 Stock-return assessment time period

In stock market investing, there are many investing approaches that yield various returns. The name of the game is to beat the market—meaning the various market indexes, like the NASDAQ, or the S&P 500. The time it takes for our portfolio return to yield enough data for a meaningful comparison to a benchmark is a key consideration. For it determines the *minimum length of time* we have to wait to see if the approach we have chosen performs favorably or not with respect to a benchmark, say the S&P 500 index.

We can monitor the return of our portfolio hourly, daily, weekly, monthly, quarterly, etc. The closer in time we look, the more wiggles we see in the return signal. Noise is what we mostly see. There is a time period where various returns can be meaningfully compared.

Assessment time period: about three years

What is this time period? There is no hard and fast rule in determining this time period. Conventional wisdom says it is about three years. This means if you adopt an investing approach, it takes about three years for the merits or demerits of the approach to emerge. This means, no matter what happens to the stock market, however your portfolio performs, do not change your approach, before the end of the three-year period. If you do, then you will not be able to meaningfully assess the merits of the approach you have chosen.

The mismatch of our emotional time horizon with the stock-return assessment time period is a source of problems to many investors. The fact is that our psychological time horizon is very much shorter than the stock return assessment time period. It is even much shorter compared to the ideal investment time horizon—20, 30, 40, 50 years, or more. The fact in itself is not the problem. It is what you do with it that causes troubles.

1.3 Problems arising from short-time horizon

First, our short time horizon induces **impatience** from the seeming eternity of wait. Three years wait is an awfully long time compared to a day. Investors who are not aware of the notion of stock-return assessment time period will flit from one investing approach to another; or from one mutual fund to another—to the detriment of their pockets. Their criterion for switching is no more robust than the adage: the grass is greener in my neighbor's lawn. To those who are aware, many will lose confidence in the idea when they see negative returns in their portfolio; and eventually abandon the idea and chase the "hot" index, or the "hot" mutual fund, or the "hot" manager. "Chasing" anything "hot" is not a viable investing approach.

Second, our short time horizon sets our mind to think of investing as a quick "fix", where we gain quick profits to pay for a car or a house. In this frame of mind, investing will last at least a few months, at most a few years. What I have just described is not investing, but speculating. Speculation is not what this book is about. But, people conflate the two. So, someone with a short time horizon and invests accordingly will eventually find the stock market as capricious as a prima donna—there is no rhyme or reason.

Third, our short time horizon encourages the hit-and-run activity in the stock market, what is formally called *trading*. To put it differently, you cast your bait and immediately reel in the catch. It is possible to make money in the stock market by trading. It is equally possible to lose money by trading. Trading is not what this book is about. Trading is not investing. So, someone who engages in trading will eventually find the stock market purely a random process—equally, there is no rhyme or reason.

1.4 What stock investing is all about

Fourth, most important of all, our short time horizon makes it difficult for us to see what investing in stocks is all about. Investing in stocks is not a quick "fix". Nor, is it a hit-and-run affair. Neither is it speculation or trading. It is a long-term or a permanent activity, where your money grows over time powered by compounding; at a certain point in time you can start withdrawing money at set limits at set frequency, leaving the core investment to continue to grow for a long, long time. This is my ideal definition of stock market investing. This is what Warren Buffett and the great masters are and were doing.

Let me take the time to unravel this definition. Let's first discuss **permanence** or a very long time. You may quip there is nothing permanent in this world. Yes, I agree. But, there are many things that are close to permanent. Say, the institution of marriage is one. Another is religion. Viewing your core investment as **permanent** or for a very long time induces a completely different attitude in making investing decisions. To your short time horizon, this view may not make sense. I hope in the course of this book, you will come around.

1.5 Allowing full power of compounded growth

The decision to go for *permanence* or a long time horizon is based on capturing the full potential of the power of compounding. The rate of growth of your money increases with time. Putting it differently, the growth of your money accelerates with time—the longer, the greater the acceleration. To my mind, the minimum time to hold a portfolio of stocks is 20 years (see chapter 6 for the reason).

The best way to think about compound growth is your self-growth. A full grown you has about 37.2 trillion cells.

Simplifying the complex situation, by simply asking approximately how many cell divisions you underwent to make you. Doing the calculation, we get about 45 cell divisions. From a microscopic fertilized egg, it took the egg just 45 cell divisions to make you.

In the same way, a small amount of money in 40-45 years of compound growth will balloon to a huge amount, like you from a microscopic size ballooning to an adult human in merely 45 cell divisions.

At a compounded annual growth rate of 12%, (the average return of the S&P 500 index is about 12%), an investment of $5,000 at this rate will become $465,255 in 40 years. At the compound rate of 17%, $5,000 will become $2,669,344 in 40 years. That's a lot of growth of your money!

There is a point in time when the annual incremental growth of your money is bigger than your annual expenditure. At this point, you can start to withdraw a set amount, say your quarterly expenditure, leaving a core amount that continues to grow for a long time.

A very important question

At this point, you are probably uneasy. What about the market crash of 2007-2009, you may ask? Does a market crash not nullify everything I have just said? This is a very important question. We will answer this question in Part 3, chapter 13, *Managing our Portfolio.*

Summary

In resume, our short time horizon tends to make us abandon the idea of stock-return assessment time period—about three years—which sets the minimum period of wait for the investing approach we chose to show its merits, thereby meaningfully assess it against a benchmark, like the NASDAQ index. Abandoning the idea of return assessment time period, we flit like a butterfly from one approach to another, chasing the "hot" approach or the "hot" fund manager.

Our short time horizon tends to make us see investing as a quick "fix" to make profits, say, to pay for a car. This is speculation not investing.

Our short time horizon disposes us to engage in a hit-and-run activity or formally known as trading. Trading is not investing.

Most important of all, our short time horizon prevents us from seeing the long-time nature of stock investing—20, 30 years or more—where the long time allows the compounded growth to do its magic, as well as greatly increases our probability of success of substantial gains.

Chapter 2: Poor Intuitive Statistician

Our instinct for understanding events involving randomness or chance is very poor—almost non-existent. In contrast, our sensitivity to events involving causes is honed to the extreme such that, in modern times, it is equally problematic in some circumstances. In this chapter, we examine the consequences of this double deficiency—of too little understanding of chance events and of too much sensitivity to causal events. The asymmetry has significant implications in our expectations of stock returns, in our investment decisions, and in how we deal with 20% or more declines of the stock market.

2.1 Ultra-sensitivity to causal events

Our ancestors in the savannahs in Africa paid close attention to the rustling of leaves. They could pay dearly with their lives if they ignored the rustle as just caused by a random fluctuation of the wind. They were keenly attuned to causes—intentional causes. Their survival and thus their ability to pass on their genes depended on such keen awareness.

They navigated in a reality teeming with intentional agents—predators, intent on turning them to protein sources; or foes of their kind out to get them in a fight for food, mate, territory or supremacy. To drop their vigilance to "causes" was to invite the end of their line.

Thus, we evolved into superb intuitive "causaliticians"; but, very poor intuitive statisticians. Eons of time honed our ancestors to be sensitive to causal events; but not to chance events. Our mind structure is such that for any event we automatically search for its cause. We expect there to be always some correspondence between events and causes.

2.2 Ultra-sensitivity to causal events: effect on decisions

When confronted with statistical fluctuations in occurrences, what baffles our mind is this: there is no identifiable cause or causes. Yet, even in the absence of cause, we see effects occurring. Since we were honed over eons of time to act to stop the cause from effecting the undesired result, even in the absence of identifiable cause, we tend to do something—anything—in the hope that the mere acting could somehow thwart the cause from continuing to produce the undesired effect.

To be specific, our ultra-sensitivity to causality sets us to expect a cause for every event. It follows that a drop in the return of our portfolio must have a "cause". But, we have no idea what it is. The following day our portfolio continues to bleed. Our level of anxiety goes up. We become more edgy. The fact drives us to conjure up causes. We conjecture, say, our choice of the stocks with prices dropping in the last two days is a mistake. So we decide to drop these stocks and replace them with the alternatives in the list we use in the original purchase.

We do the "purge"—out go the "undesirables"; in come the "desirables". At first, we congratulate our egos; we puff our chest for being right in our hunch. A week or two later, the green numbers in our portfolio turn into red.

And the round of searching for a "cause" for a drop in return is on again. It is always on. As we will see in the last section and in section 3.3, the search for reasons or causes for the fluctuations in our returns is a misplaced concern. We will indicate what concerns should replace it.

All these searches arise from our inherited trait of ultra-sensitivity to causality, as well as our dismal lack of sensitivity to chance events. This brings us to the topic of the next section.

2.3 Lack of sensitivity to chance events

On the other hand, unfortunately, we have not learned an iota of statistical reasoning in the evolutionary "Garden of Eden", in the savannahs in Africa. What baffled our ancestors and still baffles us today is when we are confronted with statistical facts that can change the probabilities of occurrences but, yet there are no "causes" to be found.

To illustrate the point above, let's discuss an example in Daniel Kahneman's book, Thinking, Fast and Slow. A survey on the incidence of kidney cancer in 3,141 counties in the United States shows a very interesting pattern: counties exhibiting the lowest incidence of kidney cancer tend to be mostly rural, sparsely populated, and located in traditionally Republican states in the Midwest, the South, and the West. If you are asked to comment, you probably would quickly dismiss the notion that Republican politics has something to do with it. You would probably proffer the notion that the rural lifestyle—clean air, unpolluted water, etc.—is the cause.

Now consider the counties with the highest incidence of kidney cancer. You will find the counties tend to be mostly rural, sparsely populated, and located in traditionally Republican states in the Midwest, the South, and the West. If you say the reason is the rural lifestyle—lack of medical facility, poor sanitation, etc., you are invoking the same reason, rural lifestyle to explain two completely different results.

What is going on here? Our minds automatically search for causes to explain the incidence, as soon as we hear the report. That is just the way our mind works: we instinctively search for causal agents.

2.4 The law of small numbers

Again, we are superb intuitive "causaliticians"; but very poor intuitive "statisticians". We are wired to see causality in events. Protest as much as we like—but, the incidence of kidney cancer reported does not have a cause. The contradictory incidence exhibited by the same type of counties is allowed for by the sampling methodology. It is allowed for by the law of small numbers; not caused by it. The smaller the sample, the less reliable is the result—huge variation is possible. The incidence result is not a "fact"; it is an "artifact" of the sampling methodology.

The statistical behavior of random events we have difficulty wrapping our minds around. The image of a hammer breaking an egg is absent in statistical events.

2.5 Lack of sensitivity to chance events: effect on decisions

Now, our ultra-sensitivity to "causes" is one side of the coin; the other side is the lack of sensitivity to "causeless" events. One side is sure a cause exists for every event; the other side does not know there is no cause for random events.

Our lack of statistical intuition, compounded by our certainty of causes, makes for a confused mind in our confrontation with the facts of our portfolio.

We tend to act on the law of small numbers, i.e. we base our decision on one event or two. When a red number appears in our portfolio, we are concerned and may take action to replace the stock in question; or change investing approach; etc.

When negative returns confront us, we are sure—so we are wired to think—the drop in our return must be due to some cause. We must do something—anything, so we are wired to act, to neutralize the unknown cause.

We intuitively feel that we will be amiss if we do not do anything. Together with overconfidence, this lack of statistical intuition is contributory to the excessive buying and selling in the stock market. Likewise, we keep "chasing heat"; abandon our investment approach too soon; and invest in and out of stocks.

All these partly arise from a lack of understanding of the nature of statistical behavior of events.

What if we are wired to intuitively understand occurrences of events that exhibit statistical behavior? What if we are wired to see many events happen without a "cause"? What if we see events occurring but no "hammers"—in contrast to an egg breaking from a striking fork?

Then, the red numbers in our portfolio are no surprise. They are just fluctuations—a natural for quantities generated by random events, just like the portfolio return.

What if we learned in the savannahs in Africa that we cannot control the statistical fluctuations in natural events, in contrast to some control we have with causal events. If we can identify the cause of an event, say a lion, then we can do something to stop the cause: there are options open to us—kill it, run away from it, etc. For quantities arising from random events, we don't even have the luxury of knowing the "cause", much less exercise some control.

Then, we do not have to do "something" to neutralize the "cause" of the drop in our return. The drop is merely statistical fluctuations we cannot control.

But, investors, in the hope to stop the perceived hemorrhaging of their portfolio, they do something—anything; instead of doing nothing. That is, continue to follow the guidelines of their chosen investment approach, if they have one.

Most of the time, the right action is to do nothing. However, for the offspring of the African savannah dwellers, the hardest thing to do is precisely to do nothing.

Furthermore, our lack of understanding of the "causeless" nature of chance occurrences, also prods us to chase the "hot" mutual fund because to our mind the "cause" of the underperformance of our portfolio is the lousy fund manager. In reality, the performance of our fund manager may in fact be stellar if assessed at the requisite time horizon. Due to statistical fluctuations, the fund was down when we viewed it. Down as well as up are allowed for by randomness. Stock returns have a random component.

This brings us to a concept underlying my view of the stock market—the two-component model of returns.

2.6 The two-component model of stock returns

We now come to the central notion that underpins everything I say on stock investing—*the two-component model of portfolio returns.*

Are stock returns purely statistical in nature? Are there no real "causes" hidden in the seemingly random wiggle of stock returns?

Stock returns have both a causal, as well as a chance component. Stock returns are like currents in a wire. A current essentially consists of a flow of electrons from one point in a wire to another. Let's follow an electron among the billions that constitute a current. The said electron undergoes random motion due to heat, forward-backward along essentially one dimension. But, superimposed on its thermal random motion is an overall drift in the direction opposite to the applied potential difference or voltage. It is the applied external force that causes the overall drift—in a given direction—of the random motion of the electrons in a wire.

Stock return like a current consists of a random and a causal or "drift" component. The random component consists of the buying and selling of shares of stock by millions of investors daily, in varying amounts at varying times, worldwide. These random transactions give rise to the random up and down movement in value of returns. But, superimposed on the random up-down movement in value is an overall drift upward—more buy than sell—driven by the anticipation by investors of share-price appreciation in the future, based on the perception of the trending growth of the economy; by the growth of the business of the company underlying a specific stock. That's why the stock market is a leading indicator of the Economy. It swings up about six months before the Economy does; and conversely—it swings down before the Economy hits a lowest point.

Does anybody need to know the details of the impact on stock returns by all the millions of events occurring daily? And even granted that we can know that, does it avail us anything? It avails us nothing. What we get, if we can hear the information, is the endless hiss of noise.

Translated in terms of our portfolio, the up-down random motion of stock returns we can safely ignore.

To repeat, the overall drift of stock returns upward is causal: the driver is the anticipation of share-price appreciation, based on perceptions of the trending growth of the economy; in particular, the growth of the company underlying the stock. Both growths, in turn, are driven by increasing demands for goods and services, which in turn drive technology innovations—all these arise from the growth of population. The growth of demand due to the growth of population is the ultimate cause of the upward drift of stock returns.

In the end, the stock market is all about the prices of shares of stocks. And ultimately, just like the prices of any commodity, as we all learn in Economics 101, prices of shares of stocks depend on the supply and demand for those shares. In the short term, the supply of shares is constant. The time horizon for the supply of new shares is long—in years. The creation of new shares by the process of an IPO, initial public offering, of a new company goes through many steps set by Government regulators. The time to complete the requirements is in years. Also share buybacks by companies and mergers of companies to reduce the number of shares have a time period in years. That's the supply side.

The demand side has both a short time component and a long time component. The psychological disposition of an investor at a given moment may prod her to buy or sell shares of company XYZ. Perhaps, the news on the housing market sways her to buy or sell. The short-time wiggles in stock prices arise from such purchases or sales. Other investors, on the other hand, who are attuned to the goings on in the supply side, may buy or sell stocks accordingly. Still other investors examine the overall outlook of the economy to inform their buy and sell of stock shares. Such purchases or sales from these investors shape the long time component on the demand side.

The bottom line: stock returns wiggle randomly in the positive and negative direction; nevertheless, superimposed on the random wiggling, is an overall drift upward, just like an electron in a current has an overall drift velocity in a given direction.

2.7 Statistical nature of stock returns: effects on decisions

Someone who is aware of the random behavior of stock returns makes decisions differently from one who is not. A key decision she makes, informed by her understanding of the random behavior of stock returns, is to invest for a long time period—the longer, the better. In a short period of time, the random fluctuations mask the drift return signal. The cumulative return signal even at a compounded rate of growth, may not have enough time to come out above the random noise. This fact is the basis for: as the holding time increases, the probability of losing money decreases.

Putting it differently, statistical analysis of stock returns shows the longer the time, the greater is the probability of a positive return. Remember that investing in the stock market is a probability's game—and neither a certainty's game; nor a possibility's game.

From her understanding of the statistical nature of stock returns, she is not bothered by the daily alternations of red and green in her portfolio returns. She knows that the daily change in color is the visible random part of the stock return. She equally knows the drift part of the stock return, though invisible, is always present, growing at a compounded rate. The drift part will come out clearly in the long term. The daily gyrations of her portfolio return she views with serenity, as calmly as a Buddhist practitioner.

To repeat, the random component of returns is readily seen at the short time scale. However, the causal component is not easily visible at this scale. It is only visible when we look at returns at a long enough time scale.

2.8 Overall drift of stock returns: effects on decisions

To complement our discussion on the random part, we now take on the causal part—the "drift" part. Knowing the nature of the overall drift part of the stock return, an investor will invest for a long time period. The reason is that the rate of compounded growth grows faster, the longer the time. In terms of acceleration, the longer the time, the bigger is the acceleration. This is ideal for money that you can set aside for a long time, till your retirement.

Someone who understands the drift part of stock returns is not worried about drops in the stock market—either a correction (<20%), or a bear market (>20%). She knows the drift "force" is always present, ever busy growing at a compounded rate. Remember she does not need her money till retirement.

The last remark prompts us to raise an important question: what if the crash happens around the time of your retirement? This is another important question we will answer in Part 3 in chapter 13, Managing Our Portfolio.

2.9 Laboratory for re-programming our minds

The stock market is a wonderful laboratory for re-programming your mind to rein in your emotions. Say you understand the rationale of the investment approach you have chosen. If it is any good, a key component of any worthwhile approach is the need for a longer time horizon, say three years, for any realistic assessment of its efficacy to make sense.

So, you open an account using the approach you pick. Either you directly manage the account; or, a professional manages it as in a mutual fund. It is a testament to the level of your emotional intelligence if you can stick to your chosen approach despite what happens to your return compared to indexes or to your friends' returns.

To become a better stock investor and make money in the stock market, you have to know human nature in order to overcome its weaknesses to better manage your portfolio for a long wealth creation.

Summary

In resume, our over-sensitivity to causes combined with our lack of understanding of the statistical behavior of quantities generated by random events predisposes us to make mistakes in our investing decisions. Understanding the two-component model of portfolio returns will give us a sound basis for managing our emotions, as well as managing our portfolio.

Knowing the statistical nature of stock returns, we can sleep soundly at night, regardless of the oscillations of our returns. In fact, if a fund manager claims to the contrary, that his returns are smooth, consistent: <u>no fluctuations whatsoever, then alarm bells should ring!</u> The celebrated case of this absence of fluctuations is the notorious Madoff affair. Madoff claimed a consistent return of 10% to 12% to his clients, year in and year out. As we will see in chapter 6, Part 2, yearly returns are lumpy, swinging from a high positive of say 37%, to a low negative of say -25%. If anybody claims the contrary, right off we should run away.

The causal or the "drift" component of stock returns ought to be the focus of our concern. As we will discuss in chapter 11, Part 3, our concern should be how to optimally capture the "force" of the drift by our choice of investment approach and by the management of our portfolio.

Wherever we are in the economic cycle, the causal component, the "drift" force, is ever present, growing our return at a compounded rate, seemingly invisible in short time scales; but, gratifyingly visible in long time scales.

Chapter 3: Loss aversion

Imagine you are living in the environment where our ancestors lived. You will find an environment where pain and death are a constant. A lethal snake bite can send you writhing in pain with no possible relief; and death inevitably follows. Someone whom you love; with whom you just had a meal—suddenly meets his end. It is not a surprise to you, for death is a commonplace. Nevertheless, you feel the loss and grieve.

3.1 Pain of loss against the joy of gain

Such in brief is a possible scenario depicting the darker side of life of our ancestors, giving rise to traits we inherit, like the fear of snakes, including that of loss aversion.

The third innate trait we explore is our aversion to loss. We suffer twice more from loss than we enjoy the same amount of gain. Or, our brain is willing to pay twice more to avoid pain as to enjoy the same amount of gain. What does this have to do with stock market investing? Indeed, it has much to do with it—as we will see.

In the same way that we dread the dentist drill, so we dread the "red" numbers in our portfolio!

When stock prices go up, everybody is happy. We enjoy the gain. We feel good, as our portfolio looks like lush vegetation—green all over the page. We feel we are on top of the world. We pat ourselves in the back for being smart in our choice of stocks. For every event, there is a cause—and we are it.

The problem arises when our portfolio looks like a field of red peppers—red all around. Our instinct for causality kicks in into gear. For every event, there is a cause. But, surely we are not the cause. To attribute failure to ourselves is not the way human nature evolved. The cause is everybody or everything else, except us. To believe strongly in ourselves without qualifications was a necessity in the unforgiving world of our ancestors. How else could our ancestors summon up the courage to face off a mammoth predator without overconfidence in their prowess in a game of win or death? A sense of failure is absent when the outcome is either life or death.

Facing a seeming adversity of negative returns, we hold ourselves blameless, enabling us to go on investing. We point our accusing fingers elsewhere and not to us.

Our natural aversion to loss joins in. We are in a state of agitation; anxiety. We become edgy. We feel we have to do something. We are concerned that the slight drop today would continue. A focus of our worry is our "winners". Who knows if they too will turn from "green" to "red" tomorrow, or the day after tomorrow? On account of this uncertainty, we now seriously entertain the idea of selling our winners, to forestall losing all the gains accumulated so far. Or, to use the commonly used phrase—*to lock our gains.*

Our feeling it is better to sell our winners builds up. Our anticipation of the pain we will feel if our winners will lose their gains seems to seal the deal. We do not want to feel the pain of losing what we already have. A bird in the hand is better than two in the bush, we remember.

3.2 Selling our winners; keeping our losers

But, we have second thoughts about selling our winners. We read somewhere that investors make the mistake of parting from winners too early cutting short what could be a long run. So, that recollection gives us pause; we are temporarily confused. We hesitate; but, eventually we sell our winners— avoidance of the pain of loss tips the balance against the joy of future gain.

We hate to view our stocks when red peppers our portfolio. We try at all cost to avoid the pain of loss. We feel admission of loss is a diminution of our ego. In our mental accounting, a loss on paper—unrealized—is not a loss. We engage in wishful thinking—nursing the hope our losers, at least some, will recover and even be in positive territory. Again, we heard or read investors tend to keep their losers too long. We feel fifty-fifty on the issue. But our gut feel breaks the tie: our losers have it.

Psychologically, we feel we don't have to acknowledge the loss until we sell the losers. So, to avoid the pain of owning up to the loss, we hide them under the rug, so to speak.

3.3 A possible antidote for loss aversion

How do we neutralize this natural loss aversion? First, knowing we are subject to it is a necessary first step. Being aware our loss aversion leads us to a poor management of our portfolio is an additional step. An understanding of the components of stock returns is a crucial step. Without this understanding, our gut reaction from loss aversion goes unchecked—when we see red peppering our portfolio.

We can greatly diminish our tendency to loss aversion by the choice of an investing approach. If we do not have a well thought through approach to investing, then we will be slaves to our emotions—anything goes. We will discuss choosing an investing approach in Part 3, chapter 11—Which investing approach?

What if we understand the two-component model of stock returns—a random component and a causal component? What if we are convinced random events by definition do not have "causes"? Therefore, we do not need to understand the random change in color from red to green to red, etc. in terms of causes; but, accept the random fluctuations in the value of our portfolio as they are. It is to be expected a quantity, like stock returns, generated by random events, must exhibit random fluctuations. It is a natural. We accept them as they are—random. Unwelcome as they may be; we accept them in the same way as we accept, say, pimples!

Then, we will not be anxious to see red in our portfolio. It is just equivalent to a coin flip—sometimes up; some of the time down. There is nothing we can do about it. Selling our winners will not make the random fluctuation in our portfolio return go away. Nor keeping our losers reduces the frequency or the amplitude of the fluctuations. The zigzag path of stock returns is exactly the same as electrons in a current in a wire.

Equally, there is nothing to fear about it. In fact, if we see "red" for days in a row, it could be the time to add positions in our portfolio since the shares have gotten cheaper. This of course depends on the investing approach we have chosen. With this new pair of eyes, we may even look forward to "red" days as buying opportunities—not days to dread; nor days to sell our winners.

Further, what if we are convinced of the overall upward drift component of stock returns? Though invisible in a short time period, we are convinced the drift component is always present, moving upward at compounded rate of growth. What if we are convinced that the longer the time period, the greater is the visibility of the cumulated growth arising from the drift?

Then, with this added perspective, we clearly see that our concern for the fluctuation in stock return value is misplaced. It should not be a concern at all. What counts is the ever present drift "force" that drives the upward trend of stock returns, which grows at a compounded rate of growth. Instead of the useless worry on the fluctuations, our concern should be: (1) what should be the investing approach to choose to optimally capture the upward drift "force"; and (2) how should we manage our portfolio to optimally ride the drift "force.

These are precisely the concerns we will address and other related issues in Part 3, chapter 11—Which investing approach; and chapter 13—Managing our portfolio.

Summary

So, loss aversion emotionally prods us to do two things that detract from our goal in stock investing: (1) it goads us to prematurely sell our winners; and (2) it tricks us to keep our losers—by not selling our losers we psychologically avoid the pain of owning up to a loss.

Our understanding of the two-component model of stock returns would greatly enhance our ability to educate our emotions. The random component makes us realize there is no need to worry or dread the red numbers in our portfolio. They are to be expected. They are just random fluctuations. They add up to zero.

What should be the focus of our attention is the drift or causal component. They sum up over the long term to the total gain or profit of our investment.

Chapter 4: Envy and Herd Mentality

The recent discovery of mirror neurons opens up possibilities of understanding at the molecular level many of our day-to-day behaviors—empathy, imitation, autism, intentionality, etc. Mirror neurons are ones that fire when you see actions done by others, as when you do the action yourself. I suggest that envy and herd mentality might involve mirror neurons in their initiation.

This brings us to the traits of envy and herd mentality, the subject matter in this chapter.

Envy can be a force for good or for bad. Say, you envy your friend because he is well known for his success in the theater. This sets you up to work hard to attain the same thing, if not surpass your friend's achievement. If, on the other hand, your envy makes you mad and sets you off to spread falsehoods about your friend to destroy his reputation, then your envy is a negative force.

4.1 Envy—a force for wealth destruction

How is this relevant to stock market investing? The first case of envy above is positive—a force for good in ordinary circumstances. But, in the stock investing world, envy that sets you to follow others is a negative force. It is a force not for wealth creation; but, for wealth destruction.

To emulate others' portfolio by abandoning your chosen approach is not good for your wealth. Switching investment approach before the return assessment time horizon is over is not good for wealth creation.

A study over a twenty-year period ending in 2009 on stock investors who owned stock portfolios in ETF or mutual funds—has revealing results. First, their average return over the twenty-year period was a low of 3.2%. Over the same period, the S&P 500 index averaged 8.2%. That is a full 5% lag, a huge underperformance when we view its implication in a long time horizon. Second, over the twenty-year period in the study, the average holding time of investors in ETFs or mutual funds is 3.2 years. Investing for 3.2 years in ETFs or mutual funds does not make sense—as we will see in chapter 6. The longer the holding period, the more investing in stocks makes sense, whether in ETFs or mutual funds or individual accounts.

How do the revealing findings relate to envy? When we see a friend's portfolio return higher than our own, we naturally feel a loser. Our envy prods us to at least equal it by imitating her portfolio. When we see the NASDAQ index perform better than the S&P 500 index, we switch to an ETF or mutual fund that emulates the NASDAQ. This in and out activity degrades the returns and explains the short holding period.

As we saw in the twenty-year study, the short holding period of 3.2 years meant a return of 3.2%, a full 5% lag from the S&P 500 index return of 8.2% over the same period.

4.2 Mouth of a huge crocodile

Many of us may have seen the great Serengeti wildebeest annual migration on TV. Every year a vast number of wildebeests—a herd—timed to coincide with rainfall and grassland growth, gather together to search for fresh grazing and water. Many of them, unsuspecting, fall victim to predators—like crocodiles.

It seems the same pattern holds with investors. A herd of investors, in search of fortune, manages to act in concert whenever the stock market is in a bull run. The wildebeests get their timing right. For the herd of investors, they get their timing all wrong—it is for disaster; not for fortune.

As we see others loading up on stocks, we too max out our holdings with stocks. As we noted above, the timing is all wrong—the overall stock valuation is high. As members of the herd, we buy shares above average prices. Unbeknownst to us, anytime now, the bubble will burst. And when it does, we are like the wildebeest jumping into the water only to land into the mouth of a huge crocodile!

4.3 Antidote for envy and herd mentality

What could we do to counter our tendency to envy and herd mentality as applied in stock investing? As with the other traits, one, awareness is the first step. Two, a most important step is to understand the two-component model of portfolio return. Three, another important step is to choose the investing approach that is emotion-proof as humanly possible. This will be a topic in Part 3, chapter 11—Which investing approach?

What if we understand that stock returns have time scales in decades, not in years – as we will argue in section 6.1? So, when we envy the return of our friend for a period of a week, a month, a quarter, or a year—we are envious really about nothing. The returns at this period do not mean anything. They are mainly statistical fluctuations.

We find our envy is baseless. We now realize the change in our portfolio to imitate our friend's is unwarranted. Moreover, it is precisely the reason why investors have significantly lower returns than the S&P 500 return.

What about the herd mentality? What can we do to hold our "urge" to follow the herd? The first thing I suggest is the following. When we feel the urge to follow the herd, think of the gaping mouth of a huge crocodile. That is where our hard-earned money goes!

We noted above the herd of investors gather at a time near the top of a bull run. It is precisely the time when the prices are bloated. One of the considerations in understanding portfolio returns is the issue of how to ride the "drift" force optimally. One way to optimize our ride with the "drift" force is to go by the idea of "paying a lot less" for the stocks we include in our portfolio. It rests on the fact that "the price we pay determines the return we get".

With this mindset, we will not be inclined to follow any herd. As we will see in Part 3, chapter 11, to implement the idea of "pay a lot less", Prof Joel Greenblatt has developed a methodology in determining the rankings of companies from which to choose. If we adopt this methodology in our choice of what to include in our portfolio, then the temptation to follow the herd is minimal or absent.

Summary

In resume, envy induces us to imitate the portfolio of other's, which by chance happens to perform better than our own; or, to change approach when other approaches by chance have a higher return than our own.

The herd mentality seduces us to do what others are doing near the top of a bull run. It is a self-defeating behavior. It could lead to a permanent loss of our investment capital.

A possible antidote suggested, besides awareness of such tendencies, is an understanding of the two-component model of portfolio return. Realizing the drift component of returns have a long time horizon; and what we see and feel in the short term is the random component of returns—we now know changing portfolio for reasons based on the random behavior of returns does not make sense.

We learn our focus of concern is how to ride the "drift" force to optimize our return. This concern will preoccupy us and not what other people do.

Chapter 5: Fear and Greed

Fear and greed, like the other traits, have both positive as well as negative roles in life. Fear is the spring to action when we are in danger. On the other hand, in pathological form, fear could freeze us into paralysis, even in largely benign circumstances.

Greed prods us to make provisions for tomorrow. On the other hand, if unmitigated, greed is a cause of strife in communities, big and small.

5.1 Zero-sum game

In stock investing, fear and greed equally play a dual role—in a game of zero-sum. Investors with above average emotional intelligence or EQ gather the positive sum. On the other hand, those with below average EQ gather the negative sum. We will discuss the zero-sum-ness in the stock market in more detail in section 13.1

If we follow the share prices of companies over the course of a year, we notice share prices could swing wildly, say, below 50% of their starting price. We may ask: is this reasonable? Is the reality of the company behind the stock shares that much altered in terms of its fundamentals? Have the fundamentals deteriorated to below 50% to what it was at the starting date?

The answer is no. The swing comes from Mr. Market, the metaphor that Benjamin Graham used to explain the Psychology of investors in the stock market. Mr. Market is a very emotional investor. Some days he is pessimistic and fearful. He unduly undervalues stocks and sells his stocks at such a low price out of fear. On other days, Mr. Market is optimistic and greedy. He unduly overvalues stocks and happily buys the shares on offer out of greed.

The swing in share prices is the swing of the psychological disposition of Mr. Market. The emotional pendulum swings from the extremes of fear and greed.

5.2 Emotions of fear and greed

The twin emotions of fear and greed can be as devastating as a hurricane or a tsunami. When fear grips a crowd, like in a theater when someone shouts "fire", "fire", a stampede for the exits usually ensues, resulting in deaths due to trampling as chaos builds up, or death by smoke inhalation; or death by fire.

When fear grips investors in the stock market, it could send tsunami waves across the stock market around the world—laying waste years of accumulated savings. The tsunami waves of fear would not be there, if mounds of shares at sky-high prices were not built-up by the other emotion of greed.

Near the top of a long bull run, out of greed, we forget that there are dark clouds behind the silver lining. We pile up to buy shares at bloated prices. Valuation is no longer important. We load up, so to speak, our trucks and SUVs full of shares of stocks. Unsuspecting the fall is imminent—we wax euphoric at the huge gains our portfolio has been racking up.

Then, a drop in prices begins. We can't believe it. We hold on. The stock market continues its decline. Out of fear, panic selling starts. Like in the 2007-2009 bear market, the decline can go to depths that we cannot take any more. Fear sets a massive sell-off.

5.3 This time is different

Having gone through such "carnage", we vow never again to buy shares of stocks. But, it seems our memory is short. The pain of loss with time seems to fade. The stock market recovers and is on the way to a higher peak. Our instinct of greed gets the better of us with the rationale taken with great confidence that *this time is different.* True, the years are different. But, the forces at work—the *psychology* of people—are the same.

The results are predictable. The *boom* followed by *bust* is a cycle that occurs with clockwork regularity.

5.4 Antidote to fear and greed

What can we do to counter fear and greed? The best antidote to fear and greed is to follow an investing approach. We have to study the approach we choose inside out. Only when we are convinced of its merits do we decide to adopt it. Once we choose an investing approach, then issues of fear and greed become a non-significant issue—even a non-issue. We will spend time in Part 3 to spell out ways to overcome our biases, including fear and greed.

Summary

Fear and greed are the twin emotions, possibly leading us to decisions resulting in permanent loss of capital. Greed is the push to load up on stocks near the height of a bull run. Fear is the trigger to join a massive sell-off during a bear market. The two actions together combine to make great wealth transfers from the poor to the rich possible.

My personal suggestion to help investors not succumb to fear and greed, aside from having an explicit investing approach, is to picture a poor man who gives the little that he has to a rich man. That poor man is you when you follow greed to buy stocks at bloated prices and sell them dirt cheap out of fear.

Part 2: IQ—Understanding Stock Investing

This book, *"IQ plus EQ: The Arrow and the Hoisting Crane"*, rests on the assumption it shares with behavioral economics that real humans behave not with perfect rationality error-free—all IQ—but only with reasonableness error-prone—EQ with support from IQ.

There is a minimum IQ and EQ to be successful in stock market investing. As we have seen in Part 1, what may derail an investment approach is not the lack of IQ; but, the lack of EQ.

As we will see in the Conclusion, the level of intelligence required to be a successful stock investor is the IQ needed to understand any investment approach in terms of—the margin of safety made available by Mr. Market's fear and greed, and the purchase of good companies at below average prices; as well as the statistical nature of stock returns.

This part focuses on what our IQ needs to understand—the requisite notions for investing in the stock market: the nature of portfolio return arising from the reality of the stock market in chapter 6; the difficulty in valuing a business and an indication how to circumvent valuing a business, yet attaining the same result—paying a lot less—in chapter 7; mutual funds in terms of the margin of safety and the purchase of good companies at below average prices in chapter 8; and the arguments for value-weighted index based on Greenblatt's investing approach in chapter 9.

From essays for my sons to a book

To the young readers, who have long time horizons, it is my sincere hope while you are young and healthy that you take the opportunity to build a sizable nest egg for your retirement in your golden years. Mathematically, a compounded growth, like the stock market returns, accelerates faster the longer the time. Above a certain number of years—40 years is my choice—

a small amount of money could grow to a HUGE amount, such that it could continue to grow even after you start withdrawing money from it within limits.

To the rest of the readers, who have time horizons of 20 years or more, it is equally my sincere hope that this book will inspire you to participate in the worldwide financial transactions that help give birth to new companies, ever improving the production of goods and services, while at the same time sharing in the wealth created.

Not everybody likes to pick stocks. As the saying goes, different strokes for different folks. However, there is good news for those who do not have the inclination to pick stocks. We will see in chapter 8 and 9, mutual funds using a value-weighted allocations of stocks in a portfolio perform significantly better over funds using all other ways of allocations. The difference makes a big impact on your nest egg due to compounding over a long time till your retirement.

The virtue of mutual funds is that you are able to share in wealth creation, while pursuing full time your chosen career. In studies conducted by Prof Joel Greenblatt, he demonstrated, by back-testing using the historical data of 3,500 companies in the US, dating back to 1988, that value-weighted index, based on his method of combined ranking, beats the returns of S&P 500 by about 5 points every year. See chapter 8 and 9. That is a huge difference in the context of compounded growth over a long period, say over 40 years.

I learned it the hard way. I have passed on the insights I learned to my three sons in the form of essays. I have re-worked my essays into a book format for a wider readership. To anyone who is interested, I am proud to share with you the insights I shared with my three sons, so that you too will be able to spend your golden years with ease and comfort financially.

Chapter 6: Nature of Portfolio Returns

Portfolio return is the sole reason why we invest in the stock market in the first place. We put money in expecting gains will accrue in the future. Reality, however, demands we match our expectation with the requisite understanding. Short of that understanding, our expectation or dream turns into a nightmare!

Thus, understanding the nature of portfolio returns arising from the reality of the stock market is crucial and indispensable. Investing without such understanding is like searching a treasure in a maze blindfolded.

In this chapter, we will go rock-bottom: the bare-bones reality of the stock market. We will let the stock market speak for itself through the data. We will argue time investment horizon is 20 years or more. We will construct in detail a *two-component model of stock returns* by analyzing the "forces" driving the stock market. We will formally enunciate *"the law of long times"* that governs stock market returns.

6.1 Investment time horizon

Determining the investment time horizon is the first step when considering investment in the stock market. It will inform our expectation on the profit that will accrue. We have to insure the time we set is long enough: (1) so the probability of losing money is vanishingly small; and (2) the compounded growth rate can do its magic to make significant gains.

There is such a thing as an "objective" investment time horizon. To find it, we ask reality—by letting the stock market speak to us about her nature, through the returns of the S&P 500 index in Table 1. A key question we ask the data is: *how long should our investment time horizon be to match the nature of the reality of the stock market?*

This is a most important question. We want to settle in our minds what it means to invest in the stock market.

Suppose we invest our money for one year. Does this make any sense? Well, let's look at reality as represented by S&P 500 index returns in Table 1. If we invest in one of the years in Table 1, we will get different results. Say, if we invest in 1988, we hit a sizable return of 16.60 %. If we invest in 1989, we hit a jackpot return of 31.7 %. If we invest in 1990, we lose -3.1 %. If we invest in 1995, we hit another jackpot of 37.6 %. If we invest in 2002, we lose -22.1 %.

Table 1: S&P 500 Returns	
1988 16.60%	**1997** 33.40%
1989 31.70%	**1998** 28.60%
1990 -3.10%	**1999** 21.00%
1991 30.50%	**2000** -9.10%
1992 7.60%	**2001** -11.9%
1993 10.10%	**2002** -22.1%
1994 1.30%	**2003** 28.70%
1995 37.60%	**2004** 10.90%
1996 23.00%	**CAGR** 12.40%

Notice the returns are not varying smoothly; rather they are lumpy. This lumpiness we directly see and feel, especially when the lump is negative. A usual measure of lumpiness is the standard deviation. The set of returns in Table 1 has a standard deviation of 23.13%.

From this exercise, investing for one year, in the years shown in Table 1, we have a chance of 4/17 or 23.5 % of losing money. *Thus, investing for a year does not make sense.* One in four years, we lose money. To repeat, if we invest in and out with a holding time of one year, then we stand to lose money about once in every 4 tries.

This quick turnover of portfolios explains the significant underperformance of investors' portfolios compared to the benchmark. Investors go in and out of investing at the wrong time. Invariably, they exit in the losing years. Looking at Table 1, say, we open our fund account that tracts the S&P 500 index, on 1 January 1999. At the end of that year, we are happy with a 21% return (it is actually a little less due to fees). We feel in our bones our choice of fund is right. With great enthusiasm, we keep our account.

Table 2: CAGR over 3-year Rolling periods. S&P 500	
1990 14.17%	1998 28.26%
1991 18.53%	1999 27.56%
1992 10.81%	2000 12.25%
1993 15.63%	2001 -1.04%
1994 6.27%	2002 -14.55%
1995 15.35%	2003 -4.05%
1996 19.69%	2004 3.60%
1997 31.19%	

However, in the second year in 2000, things turn sour—a negative return of -9.1%. We hold off our thought of changing funds. We soldier on; only to find we are in a deeper hole of -11.9% in 2001. We begin to wonder why other people claim stocks are making them money. We quell a brewing disenchantment with stocks. We hold for another year. But, we run smack into a bear market. We just can't believe it—a whooping negative return of -22.1%!

This is it. Enough is enough. Without hesitation, we quit investing. By so doing we shoot ourselves in the foot by quitting in the losing year.

Table 2 contains the compounded returns over 3-year rolling periods based on data in Table 1. The rolling three-year period means 1988 to 1990, 1989 to 1991, 1990 to 1992, etc.

We now examine the case for a longer holding time. What about holding our investment for three years? Would this make sense? From Table 2, we see 3 three-year periods, where we lose money out of a total of 15 three-year periods. We have one three-year period in five of losing money, or 1/5 or 20 %. *So, investing for three years does not make sense either.* The probability of losing money slightly decreases from 23.5% for one-year holding time to 20% for three-year holding time.

Notice the variability of returns in Table 2 goes down: it is now 12.91%. Time reduces the lumpiness of returns. It is about half the variability compared to Table 1.

What about holding our investment for 5 years? Does this make sense? From Table 3, we see 2 five-year periods where the returns are negative out of 13 five-year periods. There is a chance of 2/13 or 15.4 % of losing money. *So, investing for five years does not also make statistical sense.*

The variability of returns in Table 3 further goes down to 8.76%. The probability of losing money decreases from 20% for three-year holding time to 15.4% for a five-year holding time. As the holding time increases, both the variability as well as the probability of losing money decreases.

Table 3: CAGR over 5-year Rolling periods. S&P 500	
1992 14.19%	1999 23.76%
1993 12.37%	2000 20.62%
1994 8.42%	2001 13.54%
1995 9.39%	2002 4.50%
1996 10.55%	2003 -5.47%
1997 13.55%	2004 -4.30%
1998 17.99%	

Expanding the dataset

We move on with our argument, using the return data of the S&P 500 index from Yahoo Finance, from 1950 to 2009. As investors, the signal we are most interested in is the signal of our investment returns. This signal is inevitably mixed with noise. The three Figures below are the results of my computer runs, in 2010-11, of the S&P 500 index returns excluding the dividends. The returns indicated here are purely from price appreciation. Total return is price appreciation + dividends.

The daily returns from 1950 to 2009, plotted in Figure 1, show the seeming symmetry of the positive values vis-à-vis the negative values of the S&P 500 return, with respect to the horizontal axis.

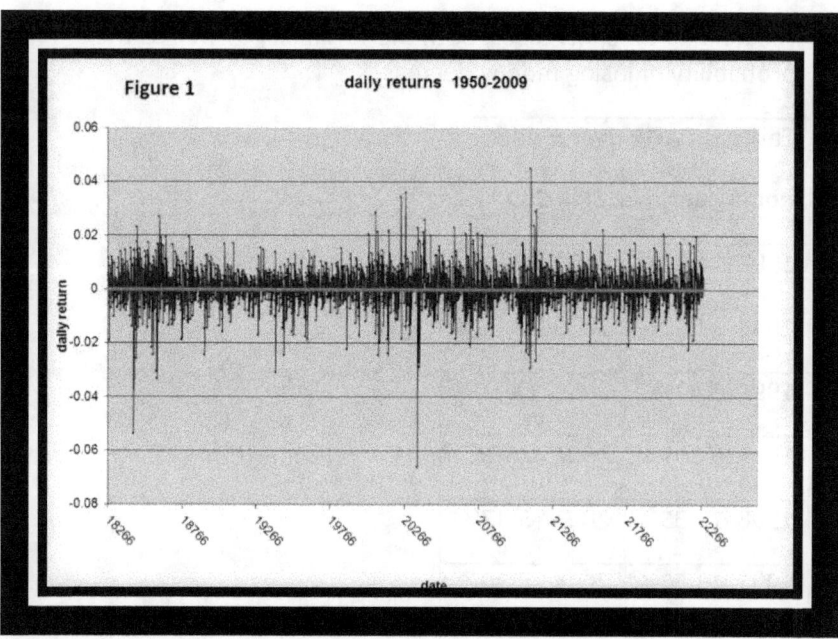

At first glance, the return seems purely random. But, if you stare intently, you will discern an overall positive return. There are more "dark" regions above the zero horizontal axis than below. The relatively larger dark area above the horizontal axis is what gives away the upward drift.

Figure 1 shows what the day-trader is playing with—the almost random movement up and down of the return. He is hoping his trade for the day is positive rather than negative. This is not investing. This is betting in a Casino, as we remarked in chapter 1.

If our holding time is a day, we are day-trading. Will you be comfortable investing in S&P 500 index fund, basing your decision on Figure 1? I bet you won't. The upward drift of the return is not clear.

Figure 2 depicts the one-year returns over 1950-2009. The return signal comes out much clearer—it is overall predominantly positive, with negative values interspersed among larger positive values. Like the data of Table 1, the 60-year dataset shows a chance of loss of 23.3%, if the holding time is one year. This just confirms our previous conclusion—one year investing time makes no sense.

To make the story short, we jump to the holding time of 20 years. Figure 3 shows returns of 20-year rolling periods over 1950-2009. The signal is very clear, indeed—the return is definitely positive, with no negative values. For this set of years, any 20-year period gets a positive return—no negative return. It

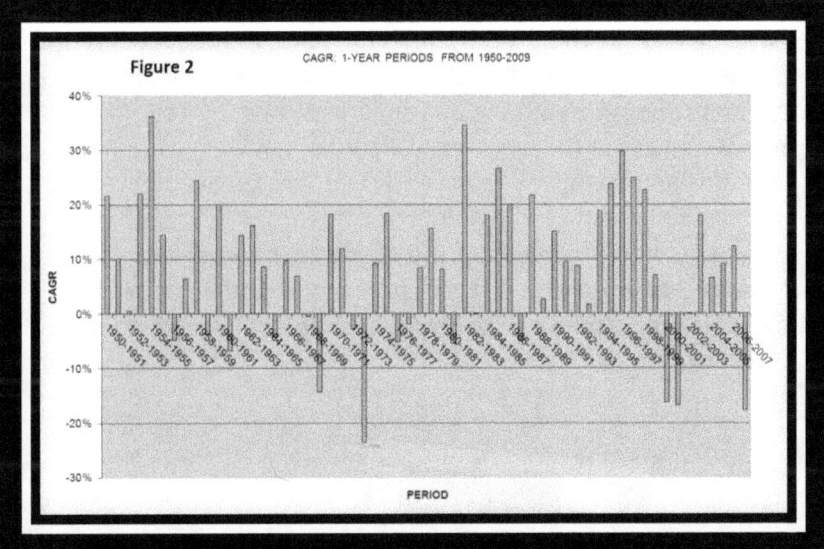

Figure 2

CAGR: 1-YEAR PERIODS FROM 1950-2009

is very highly unlikely that we will lose money if our holding time is 20 years. To me, 20 years is the cut-off time period. Any time period shorter than 20 years is not suitable for investing in stocks in proportion to its departure from 20 years.

This 20-year time is my personal cut-off period based on my own computation of returns of various rolling periods. This means if we decide to invest in stocks, we must be prepared to keep our money in stocks, rolling it forward for at least 20 years.

The 20-year result is the combined effect of random and causal "forces" in the stock market as we will see in section 6.2. We can picture 20 years as the time the upward drift—arising from causal forces—growing at compounded rate of growth wins overwhelmingly over the random forces.

Revisiting return assessment time horizon

Conventional wisdom says it takes about three years for an investing approach to demonstrate its merits or demerits compared to a benchmark. Though we showed that a three-year holding period for an investment does not make sense, nevertheless the three-year time is found to be adequate in assessing investment approaches. We have three years of return to compare with the benchmark returns. This constrains how we go about the business of insuring that we have a viable investing approach. We need to wait for three years before we can pass judgment on the merits or demerits of the approach we chose. A way to minimize the possibility of changing "horses" in mid-stream is to carefully choose the approach that best implements the two perennial principles of sound stock investing.

This puts a high premium on the selection of our investing approach.

6.2 Two-component model of stock returns

The two-component model of stock returns we construct in this section is the ground for anything we say on and do in investing. This is our guide to the stock market.

Portfolio return is like a current. Return consists of moving share prices, just like a current is made up of moving electrons. Two forces drive the electrons—the random force due to heat; and the "drift" force due to the applied potential difference or voltage. Thus, the electron motion is a composite of two kinds of motion—the random backward-forward motion along essentially one dimension; and the "drift" velocity going in one direction.

Share prices, on the other hand, are moving due to essentially two types of "effective" forces. One type is the random buying and selling of shares. The other type is the net buy of shares over the long term, with the corresponding

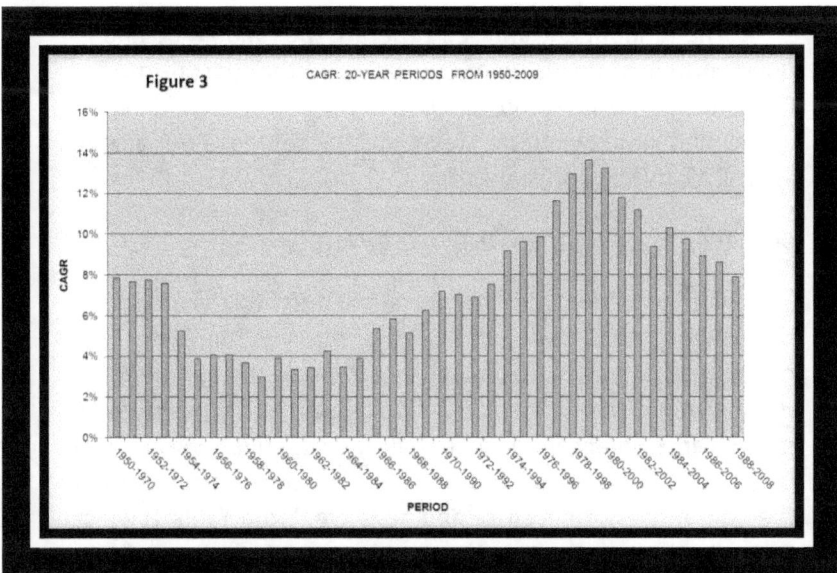

amount growing at a compounded rate. Thus, share price motion is a composite of two types of motion—the random up and down motion; and the upward exponential drift motion.

We will discuss these forces in detail below.

Random "forces" driving stock returns

The random forces give rise to the statistical behavior of returns. That's why our return fluctuates as we see in Table 1. The fluctuation goes both positive and negative. In 1990, the return is negative: -3.1%. In the following year 1991, it shoots up to +30.1%.

The buy and sell transactions by millions of investors worldwide, at different times, at varying amounts, constitute the random forces. They arise from the "heat status" of investors—hot or cold toward the shares of stocks. Though in principle, we can trace the impact of each purchase or sale on the return—in the same way we can in principle follow the impact of molecules in a gas on the walls of the container—in practice, we can only deal with the situation statistically.

The random buy and sell generate the random up and down motion of the value of our return, in the short term. Fluctuation—positive and negative—is what we see and feel daily when we view our portfolio. It is the source of our anxiety, as well as investing mistakes.

Causal or "drift" "forces" driving stock returns

On the other hand, the causal or "drift" forces produce the upward "drift" or upward trend of returns. This upward drift or trend is not obvious from Table 1. We see, though, there are more positive returns than negative ones; and the positives are mostly larger in absolute value than the negatives. Visually, the upward drift may not be obvious. But, it is there, hidden among the numbers—both positive and negative. From Table 1, we can calculate the average growth rate over the 17-year period, the so-called CAGR (compound annualized growth rate). We get 12.40%, as shown at the bottom of Table 1. This 12.40%-upward drift we have to calculate to see it.

The anticipation of share-price appreciation in the future, based on investors' perception of the upward trend of the growth of the Economy, in particular the upward trend of the growth of the business of the company underlying the stock— constitutes what I call the first level causal or "drift" force. More investors are positive about the future and thus there are more buys than sells in the long run. This difference between buys and sells, which on average over a long time is net positive, is the first level causal or drift force.

What I call the second level causal or drift force is the amount corresponding to the net buy growing at a compounded rate.

The combined action of the random wiggle and the overall upward drift motion traces a wiggly upward curve—the cumulated total amount of money in our portfolio over a long period of time.

As we discussed in chapter 2, ultimately share prices depend on supply and demand of shares.

Understanding compounded growth

We may ask: how does the "drift" component of returns grow at compounded rate. That is an excellent question. A way to understand a compounded rate of growth is to see the growth of a rabbit population starting from a rabbit pair.

We simplify the process of rabbit breeding for the purpose of this comparison. The original pair gives birth to first generation baby rabbits. Then, the original pair and the first generation give birth to next generation; and so on. After a finite number of cycles, we have a population of rabbits exploding in number.

When we have a quantity that grows in proportion to itself; and itself consists of the original self + growth—then what we have is an *explosive* growth. In Finance, we call it *compounded* growth. And to sound mathematical, we call it *exponential* growth.

Understanding compounded growth may help allay some of our concerns. As we noted above, more investors are positive about the future of the world Economy. They see the future demand for goods and services worldwide will continue to grow, due to the continued growth of the world population. This implies more buys than sells; the net effect in a year, say, is positive.

In rabbit language, our original investment gives "birth" to some gains.

This net positive increment plus the original amount we roll over to the next year. In rabbit language, this is like the original pair plus the first born-litter going for the next breeding cycle. One of two things will happen—either the rolled amount gains a net positive increment, or a negative increment.

In rabbit language, the original amount + gain continue to be invested in the second year—either giving "birth" to new gains; or no gains at all, in fact losing some of the rolled amount.

Let us take the positive case first. The total amount of the first year (the initial capital plus the positive increment) produces a positive increment in the second year. And this process is repeated as long as we hold our portfolio.

And our investment money grows exactly like our simplified rabbits grow—an EXPLOSIVE growth—over time!

We now take the second case: the increment in the second year is negative. So, the total amount of the first year plus the negative increment in the second year is an amount lower than the total amount at the end of first year. We roll the smaller amount in the third year and so on.

In rabbit language, the effect of a negative return is to reduce the number of breeding rabbits, thereby reducing the cumulative total from which to continue the next cycle.

The effect of positive and negative increments— remember in the long run, the net sum is positive—what we see as we follow the return annually is a quantity that meanders up and down the return landscape. But, eventually, over the long term, say 20 years or more, the overall net effect is a bigger quantity compared to the initial amount. We can characterize the overall growth of our money, from the initial to the final, by a constant average growth rate over the total holding period— the CAGR: compound annualized growth rate of, say, 15%.

As long as more investors are optimistic about the future than pessimistic, meaning there are more buys than sells— which is a safe bet, for as long as mankind is around—then come what may, economic boom or bust, recession or depression, the stock market, a leading indicator of the Economy, like Phoenix, will rise from the ashes and ever grows as rabbits grow.

In summary, stock returns have two components—a random and a causal or "drift" exponential upward component. The random buy and sell generate the lumpy returns. We directly see and feel this lumpiness—this is what we see and feel daily in our portfolio. It is the source of grief and mistakes to many of us.

On the other hand, the net buy and the compound growth of the corresponding net amount over the long term causes the upward "drift" component. We do not see, nor feel this upward drift. The drift upward is hard to see in the short term; but, could be surprisingly HUGE over a long enough time.

Stock Return: a drunkard's walk

To get a complementary take on Cause and Chance driving the portfolio return, let's use another analogy to think about returns—a drunkard's walk.

Imagine a portfolio return as a drunkard moving along one dimension. He can move forward or backward along a line. At every step the drunkard takes, a fair coin is flipped: heads, he moves forward; tails, backward. For our purpose, the step backward is constant in length; but the step forward is longer and increases in length with time.

This analogy captures the essential elements of the stock market. The backward step corresponds to sell transaction that sends the price down. The forward step corresponds to the buy transaction that sends the price up. The forward step being longer compared to the backward step corresponds to the net buy (there are more buys than sells). The increasing forward step with time corresponds to the compounded rate of growth.

Now imagine letting the drunkard walk for a very long time. You plot his progress over time in a graph: the y-axis, the distance of the drunkard from his starting point; the x-axis, the time of his walk. We find after a long time the drunkard to be at some distance to the right of the starting point, i.e. in the forward direction.

The plot is a wiggly line that goes up and down with time; but has an overall trend of going up.

This image helps us visualize our portfolio return. We can intuitively understand why stock portfolio has its value trending up over a long period of time, in spite of corrections and crashes. We can also intuitively understand why predictions of stock returns over shorter time period are no more than guesswork.

6.3 Law of long times

In probability theory, a "law of large numbers" is one of several theorems expressing the idea that as the number of trials of a random process increases, the percentage difference between the expected and the actual values goes to zero. For example, in a coin toss, the expected value of the number of heads or tails is one-half the number of tosses. If the number of tosses is 100, the expected number of heads or tails is 50. Typically, a result could be 40 heads and 60 tails; or 55 heads and 45 tails. If we increase the tosses to 10,000, the expected number of heads or tails is 5,000. A typical result could be 5010 heads and 4090 tails. The percentage difference |5010-5000|/5000 is 0.20%, is smaller compared to the percentage difference |40-50|/50, or 20%. We clearly see that as the number of trials increases, or tosses in our example, the actual values approach the expected value.

In stock market investing, there is a law similar to the "law of large numbers". As we showed in section 6.1, as the holding time of our portfolio increases, the probability of losing money goes to zero. In one year holding time, the probability of losing money is 23.5%; in three year holding time, 20%; in five year holding time, 15.4%; in twenty year holding time, 0.00%. These numbers are based on 17-year dataset and 60-year dataset.

I formally enunciate in this book, the "law of long times": *as the holding time of portfolio increases, the probability of losing money decreases to zero.*

The "law of long times" encapsulates the statistical component, as well as the exponential drift component of returns. It will serve as one of the bases of our choice of investment approach, a restraint on our emotion, as well as a guide in the management of our portfolio.

6.4 Stock Investing: ideal for sizable nest egg

A way of looking at stock market investing is as a vehicle to make the money you save—money you do not need now; money for your future expenditures; money for your retirement—*earn much more* compared to what you get from just depositing it in a bank, while you pursue full time your chosen career.

Is that really possible? Without spending time picking stocks, and still earning more—much more—than depositing it in a bank? This can't be...there must be a catch.

Yes, there is a catch and it is this: <u>you have to leave your money invested at all times for a long time</u> no matter what happens to the world economy and the stock market—whether the economy is undergoing a recession or a depression; or, whether the stock market is crashing or not.

That's why the money you put in the stock market is money you do not need for many years, better still money you need only at retirement. With that kind of money invested in stocks, you do not need to withdraw any of it to live. So, you have no worry during a market crash, like the once-in-a-lifetime crash of 2007-2009. If you just roll with the punches, as the saying goes, the stock market will recover, as it has from one of the worst stock market crash ever.

You may ask: what happens when a bear market coincides with my retirement? We will answer this question in Part 3, chapter 13, managing our portfolio.

Typical investors, the great majority, buy shares of stocks without any idea of what they are looking for. They follow the prices of the stocks they own, daily, weekly, or monthly--and when the prices go up, they are happy; but when the prices go down, they are twice more unhappy for the same down swing as the upswing the previous day. And when there is a sizable decline in stock prices, say 10% to 20% in a day--the technical term is "market correction", they reach for the panic button. They bail out. Our brains are wired like our ancestors'. We run for our lives and ask questions later. Market corrections are normal, but our minds are not adapted to them. This scenario is for investors who pick individual stocks.

What about those who put their money in stock mutual funds? A mutual fund is an investment vehicle managed by a company where the money from many investors is pooled to buy stocks. That's why the minimum to open an account is low, like $5,000. The management team picks the stocks to include in the portfolio. The clients pay a certain percentage for the management of the fund.

For a mutual fund investor, which you will be when you open an account in a mutual fund, the typical scenario is the following. There are hundreds of mutual funds to choose from. These myriad mutual funds follow different approaches and philosophies in managing people's money. Naturally, they will yield different returns. So, after examining a number of mutual funds, you choose one and invest money in it. You monitor your account online, if the fund has that facility. After 3 months, you hear from a friend that his mutual fund account earns a return of 2.5%. You feel envious because your return is just 2.1%. You take a mental note of that fact.

In a year's time, you meet your friend again and compare notes and you get a shock of your life! His account shows a return of 15%, above the long-term historical average of the stock market 9-12%. On the other hand, your account loses money, by 3%. What in the world is my fund manager doing! By then, you are fuming mad at the management of your mutual fund and decide to pull your money and transfer it to the mutual fund your friend has an account in. Invariably, the new fund will suffer negative returns just like the other funds by the statistical nature of returns. And the same search for a better fund which by chance happens to perform well at the time you are looking—repeats. So, we flit from one fund to another. Such is the typical transaction in the mutual fund world!

Study after study shows that even with the top long-term performing mutual funds, still investors in these top mutual funds lose money because they pull their money out at precisely the wrong time, and move their money from one mutual fund to another, chasing the hot-hand management. Invariably, they pull out in years with negative returns.

Minimum long time: 20 years

How long is a long time? From section 6.1, we learn the long time starts at 20 years; the longer, the better. From section 6.3, we also learn, with the holding time of 20 years, the probability of losing money is very close to zero. The long time that is preferable is the time till you retire. Why is this, a catch? It is because the "psychological time horizon" is much shorter than the investment time horizon. In fact, our psychological time horizon is way, way shorter than the investment time horizon of, say, 30 years or 40 years.

We are not used to think in long terms. We are so used to think in short "lumps" of time.

We are not born good stock investors. Blame it on our ancestors. Their survival instincts we inherited stand in the way. We are wired to run to the hills now, and ask questions later. We give weight to what just occurred which blurs our view of the long term. We suffer loss twice more than we enjoy an equal gain, which drives us into crazy behavior when our stocks go down. People lose money, a lot of money, in the stock market, because of the mismatch between these two time horizons.

Our psychological time horizon comes from our emotions hard-wired in our brains. The investment time horizon comes from the nature of stock returns, arising from the buy and sell by millions of investors around the world.

Studies on the stock market—I may add I spent about a year in 2010-11 doing calculations and getting similar results—by experts in university business schools, calculating stock rolling averages from 1 year to 20 years using all available data on S&P 500 index: show as the time scale increases, the volatility of returns diminishes and a positive return increasingly emerges, like a lighthouse sticking out from a distance as the waves and the tossing about subside.

Statistical analysis of the stock market shows the shorter your time horizon, the higher your probability of losing money. Conversely, the longer your time horizon, the higher is the probability of growing your money.

The long-term compound annual growth rate of stock returns of the S&P 500 index is about 12%. An investment of $5,000 at this rate will in 40 years become $465,255. That's a lot of growth of your money! If you periodically add to your initial investment, your retirement nest egg will be even bigger.

Revisiting Table 1 in Section 6.1

The first thing to notice is that the yearly returns are lumpy. Looking down the two columns of returns of the S&P 500 index that serves as the benchmark for stock returns in the US, we see a 16.60% return in 1988; then the return rockets to 31% in the following year; but nose-dives to -3.1% in the next year. If you own an index mutual fund that tracks the S&P 500 returns, then in the first 2 years you will be all smiles, but the smile will turn into a long face and fear in the third year with a negative return.

But, the -3.1% return may not drive you to push the panic button. Fast forward to the 3 consecutive years of increasingly negative returns: of -9.1%, -11.1% and -22.1% in 2000, 2001, and 2002. Three years in a row of negative returns! It is the end of the world! At this point, many investors give up—they cannot take the pain anymore—and sell all their stocks, at great loss. But as you can see from Table 1, the overall compounded annual growth of the index is 12.40% per year over the 17-year period, 1988 to 2004. At the end of that period, instead of losing money like those who bail out at the wrong time, your $5,000 would have become $36,475 instead.

Chapter 7: Difficulty in valuing a business

"If you don't know the value of the business of a company, then you don't have any business investing in the stock of that company", by Joel Greenblatt in his book, "The Little Book That Still Beats the Market".

The topic, valuing a business, naturally sets you up to yawn if you are not an MBA student. Our motivation is very practical. It is to realize the extreme difficulty of valuing a business, even for the MBA's. Therefore, for us ordinary investors, we avoid the illusion of basing our investment on our ability to value a business. The whole point of this chapter is to come out convinced, though the Greenblatt quote above is true, valuing a business is beyond the ability of small investors, like you and me.

Then, why are we discussing valuation? We are discussing valuing a business, not to become experts in the said activity. Our ulterior motive is to use our understanding of valuing a business to ultimately understand and be convinced the method developed by Greenblatt circumvents the explicit valuation of businesses—yet it achieves the purpose of valuation, i.e. to pay a lot less.

Prof Joel Greenblatt published the method in two books: (1) The Little Book that still beats the Market; and (2) The Big Secret for the small Investor.

7.1 Value of a Business

Central to sound investing is to know the value of a business. Why? It's because investing is actually buying and selling businesses. Just exactly like buying and selling used cars. In the used car business, to be successful, your buying price must be lower than your selling price—the lower, the better. The difference is your gain or profit. To be a successful used car business owner, you must be able to determine the value of a used car, its fair value and buy it for a lot less. You examine the internals of the car—the engine (its compression, oil leak to the inside of the engine block, etc.), the body (corrosion of the chassis, integrity of the transmission, etc.), and the externals of the car—bent fender, a scratch, paint peeled off, etc.

Your business rests on your ability to sell the used car with profit. Here is what you do: you determine the fair value of the car and pay a lot less. A successful used car business depends only on one thing: determining the value of the car. If you could buy a car 50% or less than its fair value, then surely your business would be a success, because you could sell the car at a profit. To repeat, successful used car business is to know the value of a used car and buy it for a lot less.

7.2 Buying and Selling Shares of Stocks

Stock market investing is like a used car business. In fact, the comparison is more accurate than you suspect. When you buy shares of stocks, you do not buy the shares from the company, except in an IPO, initial public offering of shares. The company, say, Apple, does not directly benefit from your purchase. Your money does not go to Apple but to the holder of the Apple shares. The shares pass from one holder to another— just like a used car: the car ownership changes as the car is sold and bought till nobody buys it anymore.

To repeat, stock market investing is like a used car business. You buy and sell businesses. Strictly speaking, you are buying and selling shares of stocks, which translates into "you are buying and selling a fraction of the business. But the process of buying a fraction of a business is the same as buying the whole business. The ownership of a business is divided into equally priced shares. The market value of a business is the total number of shares multiplied by the price/share. So, knowing the value of a share, you know the value of the whole business, and vice versa.

Just like in the used car business, your buying price of a share of stock must be lower than your selling price of the same share of stock, the lower the better. The difference is your gain or profit. Just like the used car business, sound investing in stocks is to know the value of a business (the stock you are buying represents) and pay a lot less. There is no rational way to be successful in investing except by knowing the value of businesses that you buy. Absent this ability, you may still have success, once in a while, due to luck—but it is not reliable or sustainable.

The secret to successful investing is to know the value of the business and pay a lot less. As Prof Greenblatt stresses, if you don't know the value of a business, you don't have any business investing in the stock of the company.

The next section is where the yawn easily comes about. But have the fortitude to go through it; it is not difficult—it just does not excite us. With your understanding, you will appreciate better the difficulty of valuing businesses, and all the more reason to be impressed at the Greenblatt method of achieving the goal of valuation of "paying a lot less", without actually doing the valuation.

7.3 Determining the Value of a Business

Say you own an ice cream business. With an investment of $50,000, your ice cream business earns $5,000 in profits. For a start, let's say that you earn $5,000 every year throughout the lifetime of the business. What is the value of your business?

The value of your business is the sum total of the series of earnings over the lifetime of the business, each earning in the series properly discounted taking into account the time value of money. The value of $5,000 a year from now is not the same if you have the $5,000 now. It is less by nearly the amount of interest you could have earned by depositing it in a bank. Say, the interest is 6%.

So,

FutureValue = PresentValue * (1 + RateOfInterest)

Solving for the PresentValue, we get

PresentValue = FutureValue / (1 + RateOfInterest)

Putting in the values, we have

PresentValue = 5,000 / (1 + 0.06) = 4,717

The present value of the $5,000 earnings at the end of year 1 is $4,717. Another way of putting it is to say that with $4,717 earning 6% interest will become $5,000 at year's end.

The same procedure applied to $5,000 earnings in year 2 yields:

FutureValue = PresentValue * (1 + RateOfInterest) * (1 + RateOfInterest)

= PresentValue * (1 + RateOfInterest) ^ (2)

Solving for the PresentValue, we obtain

PresentValue = FutureValue / (1 + RateOfInterest) ^ (2)

Putting in the values, we get

PresentValue = 5,000 / (1 + 0.06) ^ (2) = 4,450

In general, for the year n, the present value of the $5,000 earnings at the end of year n is

$$PresentValue = 5,000 / (1 + 0.06) \char94 (n)$$

The present value shrinks in size as the same earnings go farther in the out years. Say at year 200,

$$PresentValue = 5,000 / (1 + 0.06) \char94 (200) = 0.043$$

The present value of $5,000 two hundred years hence is just 4.3 cents. We can see from this rapidly decreasing behavior, that the series has a finite value--what in mathematics we call the limit point of a convergent series. It can be shown in mathematics that the value of the series is given by the formula

$$PresentValue = Earnings / discount\ rate$$

$$= 5,000 / 0.06 = \$83,333.$$

If the owner of the ice cream business offers to sell you his business for $40,000, will you buy it? Since your buying price is a lot less than the fair value—less than 50%, of course you should buy it. But wait....

Recapitulation:

So, what have we achieved? We have the notion that central to investing is to know the value of a business. The value of a business is not just the earnings this year, or next year, or the next—but the sum total of the series of earnings over its lifetime, properly discounted to account for the time value of money. Just like the value of our life: it is not just what we do this year, or next year—but the total of what we do during our lifetime. We know that a business has a value. Now we know how to calculate it—in the case, which is infinitely simplified, just to get the basic idea.

Complications in the Real World

That was easy. It was meant to illustrate a simple idea: that it is possible to value a business. To start a realistic case, let us focus on the discount rate. What is the proper discount rate to use? Is 5% okay? Is 8% right? Is 12% the reasonable rate to use?

At 5% discount rate,

$$PresentValue = Earnings / discount\ rate$$

$$= 5,000 / 0.05 = 100,000.$$

The value now jumps up to $100,000. At 8% discount rate, we have

$$PresentValue = Earnings / discount\ rate$$

$$= 5,000 / 0.08 = 62,500.$$

The value now jumps down to $62,500. At 12% discount rate, we get

$$PresentValue = Earnings / discount\ rate$$

$$= 5,000 / 0.12 = 41,667.$$

What the exercise we have just gone through shows that the value of a business is very sensitive to the discount rate you use. To see another layer of simplification, we assumed the ice cream business earns the same amount every year over its lifetime. In the real world, this is not true. The earnings vary from year to year, from quarter to quarter. We have to take this into account, by using a discount rate according to our estimate of the risk the earnings will vary from what is projected. If you think the earnings will vary in the positive direction, you will use a smaller discount rate. Or, a higher discount rate if earnings will go in the negative direction. There you have a recipe for great uncertainty in the value of a business, when you factor in the risk of earnings varying from their projected value.

The clarity and certainty with which we saw the situation in the previous section with regard to deciding whether to buy or not the offered sale of an ice cream business for $40,000—simply evaporates when we take into account the variability of earnings. It is no longer the case you have a clear bargain at $40,000 price.

To realize a further layer to the simplification, we assumed the earnings do not grow with time. In the real world, companies are born, grow to maturity, amble along in old age, and die from what Schumpeter calls the "creative destruction". What growth rate will you use? It can be shown, the formula for the PresentValue, taking into account a growth rate of earnings, is

PresentValue = Earnings / (discount rate - growth rate)

At discount rate of 8% and growth rate of 4%, we obtain

PresentValue = Earnings / (discount rate - growth rate)

= 5,000 / (0.08 - 0.04) = $125,000

At discount rate of 12% and growth rate of 4%, we obtain

PresentValue = Earnings / (discount rate - growth rate)

= 5,000 / (0.12 - 0.04) = $62,500

At discount rate of 8% and growth rate of 6%, we obtain

PresentValue = Earnings / (discount rate - growth rate)

= 5,000 / (0.08 - 0.06) = $250,000

At discount rate of 12% and growth rate of 2%, we obtain

PresentValue = Earnings / (discount rate - growth rate)

= 5,000 / (0.12 - 0.02) = $50,000

Which combination of discount and growth rates to use? We are in a, well, mickey-mouse situation--sometimes, math can be comical, where the fair value ranges from $50,000 to $250,000 depending on the combination of discount and growth rates used. An objective of this exercise is to drive home the point that valuing a business is an extremely difficult exercise. But, some people can do a reasonable job of it for some businesses in some industries. But, ordinary investors, like you and me, have no chance of doing a reasonable job of valuing a business.

Summary:

What then are the points of the whole discussion?

1) Investing is buying and selling businesses

2) To be successful in buying and selling businesses, your buying price must be lower than your selling price

3) To be successful in investing is to know the value of a business and pay a lot less

4) Valuing a business is extremely difficult, especially for ordinary investors like you and me.

How do you overcome the contradictory requirement for a successful investing with the fact of the near impossibility by ordinary investors in valuing a business? The way out is contained in (3) in the phrase "pay a lot less". In other words, the price is "cheaper". We will explain this and other concepts in the following chapters. The way out involves not actually "valuing a business", strictly speaking, at all!!! A happy turn; what a relief!

Chapter 8: The World of Mutual Funds

As Joel Greenblatt lists in his book, "The Big Secret for Small Investors", there are four ways to invest in the stock market. One, you do it yourself. Trillions of dollars are invested this way. The problem with this option is that most investors have no idea how to value a company or to construct a portfolio. If you don't know how to value a company, then you don't have any business investing in that company.

Two, you hand your money to a professional money manager. Trillions of dollars are invested this way. The problem with this option is that, with fees and institutional limitations, it has most of the time no value addition. Most money managers do not beat the market. Even more important, it is more difficult to pick good money managers than to pick stocks.

Three, you invest in a mutual fund. Trillions of dollars are invested this way. The problem with this option is that, with the management fees, most mutual funds do not even match the returns of the index, like the S&P 500. Four, you invest in a value-weighted mutual fund. Not much is invested this way yet. We will show a value-weighted mutual fund beats most professional money managers and all index mutual funds, except those who follow Greenblatt's magic formula investing.

8.1 Classification of mutual funds

To introduce you to the mutual fund world, I will discuss in some details a certain classification of the stock mutual fund world, with the view of showing the best type of mutual fund to put your money in. In this first cut, there are essentially 2 categories into which all stock mutual funds fall: (1) actively managed and (2) passively managed.

Actively Managed

For a fee, from 1% to 2% of the funds in management, a manager or a team actively buys and sells stocks with the goal of beating the market, such as the S&P 500 index, or the Russell 1000 index. To make the story short, among the thousands of actively managed mutual funds, only about 30% beats the market in any 10-year period. The underperformance is due to many reasons. One reason is the management fee—by virtue of the management fee, your returns are handicapped right at the start by 1% to 2%, which translates into a substantial amount subtracted from your returns over the long term.

Passively Managed

Another name for this category is index funds. The funds in this category buy the stocks in the index that it is emulating. Say, a fund is emulating the S&P 500 index. It buys all the stocks, 500 of them, in the index. In this way, it gets the return of the index minus the fee, which is about 0.1%. Notice the fee here is less than a 10th of the fee in an actively managed fund.

We can break this category further into 4 types: (1) market capitalization weighted index; (2) equally weighted index; (3) fundamentally weighted index; and (4) value-weighted index.

The market value of a company is calculated by multiplying the total number of stock shares by the current share price. This value is the market capitalization of the company. The portfolio of a mutual fund consists of many stocks, in the dozens or hundreds. How does management allocate the pooled money from clients to the various companies chosen by management? How much money is allocated to a given stock in the portfolio is determined by weighting scheme used.

8.2 Market Capitalization Weighted Index

Suppose we have a four-company stock market, as shown in Table 1. The table lists the market capitalization and last year's earnings of the four companies.

Four Company Stock Market: Table 1

ASSUME THE STOCK MARKET HAS ONLY FOUR COMPANIES:

TABLE 1	Market Capitalization	Last Year's Earnings
Company A	$6 billion	$100 million
Company B	$3 billion	$300 million
Company C	$1 billion	$200 million
Company D	$2 billion	$400 million
Total Market Cap of All Companies	$12 billion	
Total Earnings of all Companies		$1 billion

Market-Cap Weighted Index - Table 2

TABLE 2
Company A = $6 billion / $12 billion = 50% weight in index
Company B = $3 billion / $12 billion = 25% weight in index
Company C = $1 billion / $12 billion = 8.3% weight in index
Company D = $2 billion / $12 billion = 16.7% weight in index

The market-cap-weighted index, as the name implies, weighs companies according to market cap. Here, Company A has a market capitalization of $6 billion, which is equal to 50% of the total market cap of all stocks ($12 billion).

Let's say the index mutual fund we want to invest in tracks the S&P 500 index. The daily price changes of the 500 stocks in the index are automatically reflected in the index value, because the weighting of the companies is by market capitalization, i.e. market capitalization = price per share X total number of shares. When the price of a stock rises, its market capitalization rises; similarly, when the price of a stock goes down, the market capitalization also goes down. The value of the index is the average over 500 stocks weighted by market capitalization.

To understand the implications on our returns from our investment by using an index, we have to step back a little, and consider our definition of successful investing: know the value of a company and pay a lot less. The idea of "pay a lot less" in our definition of successful investing holds true in all investing, including investing through mutual funds. The reason the majority of mutual funds do not beat the market is because they pay more, not less. Let us see how.

"Pay a lot less" is the same idea as the "margin of safety" introduced by Benjamin Graham, the acknowledged "father" of stock investing. Remember that investing is a probabilities game and not a possibilities game. By "margin of safety", Graham advises investors to buy stocks below their fair value so that they have a margin of safety, if their bet goes wrong. This is a key idea by Ben Graham, embodied in our definition of sound investing. To link this key idea to the behavior of indexes, we have to use another key idea of Ben Graham—Mr. Market, the psychology of investing, as expounded recently by behavioral economics/ finance.

In Part 1, we stress the notion humans are naturally poor investors. It is the very nature of humans to give undue weight to what just happened and to ignore the long term in his/her decisions. This made a lot of sense in the African savannah. When you hear a faint rustle of dry leaves, then, your whole attention is focused on it for possible immediate action. The long term view of how lions behave is irrelevant at the moment. Moreover, human's natural tendency to suffer loss twice more than to enjoy gain, and the natural tendency to follow the herd, both result in driving Mr. Market (represents the total universe of investors, big and small) to oversell out of fear when the going is tough, thus sending the prices unduly down; and to overbuy out of greed when the going is good, thus sending the prices unduly up.

This see-saw up and down of stock prices happens all the time. This is the behavior of the stock market over the short term. The PSYCHOLOGY OF MR. MARKET, THE CROWD PSYCHOLOGY OF INVESTORS, dictates it. The psychology of Mr. Market influences the short-term swing of stock market prices; while the fundamentals of the economy as a whole and the business fundamentals of the companies influence the long-term behavior of stock prices.

What does this have to do with the returns of an index? The returns of the four indexes we have listed have everything to do with the two key ideas above: (1) pay a lot less or margin of safety and (2) Mr. Market psychology of fear—resulting in unduly down prices, and of greed—resulting in unduly up prices. Let us see how.

Imagine a perfectly efficient market, where investors are perfectly rational and have access to perfect information, thus prices of stocks reflect the perfect information available. This means all stocks are priced at fair value. Let's set our zero at fair value—we are interested in changes in price from fair value. Let's have a horizontal line represent this fair-value situation: our zero line, where all the stocks are at fair value, where each point on the zero-line corresponds to a stock arranged in alphabetical order at equal intervals.

In the market capitalization weighted index, the index in this ideal scenario will have a certain value. Suppose, now, we let the market be as it actually is. There will be stocks among the 500 in the index, that are unduly bid up due to greed, as well as stocks that are unduly bid down due to fear. In terms of a picture, the price changes of the unduly bid up stocks are arrows pointing up from the zero line; while the price changes of the unduly bid down stocks are arrows pointing down from the zero line. What effect does this have on the market-cap weighted index? The unduly bid up stocks raise the market cap of those stocks and thus we will unduly own more of them because their weights increase.

On the other hand, the unduly bid down stocks lower the market cap of those stocks and thus we will unduly own less of them because their weights decrease. We are hit by a double whammy! This effect of owning more of unduly bid up stocks and owning less of the unduly bid down stocks is counter to the key idea of sound investing—the margin of safety or the "pay a lot less".

Overall, the margin of safety or "pay a lot less" idea implies that we should own more of the unduly bid down stocks and less or none at all of the unduly bid up stocks. The market-cap weighting has just exactly the opposite effect overall: by the very nature of market-cap weighting, it runs opposite to the key idea of sound investing.

In resume, the market-capitalization weighting doubles down on the price distortion by Mr. Market, by owning more of the unduly bid up stocks, at the same time owning less of the unduly bid down stocks. The very procedure is contrary to the "pay a lot less" principle or the "margin of safety" principle. Any weighting scheme that is independent of prices will result in improvements in the return.

The great majority of index mutual funds are market-capitalization weighted. Now you realize that the majority of investors are "shooting" themselves in the foot, by investing in market-cap weighted index mutual funds. By investing in value-weighted funds, which will be discussed in chapter 9, you will avoid "shooting" yourself in the foot.

How can we improve the weighting procedure? What about giving equal weight to the companies? We go to the next section.

8.3 Equally Weighted Index

Equally Weighted Index - Table 3

Company A = 25% weight in index

Company B = 25% weight in index

Company C = 25% weight in index

Company D = 25% weight in index

The equally weighted index weighs all companies equally, regardless of size. Here, there are four companies in the stock universe, and therefore each gets a one-fourth weight in the index.

Again, we have a 500-stock portfolio. Giving equal weight, each stock will have a weight of 1/500 or 0.2%. We expect overall that the over-weighting of unduly bid up stocks and the under-weighting of unduly bid down stocks, still occur but not systematically arising by the very procedure, as is the case with market-cap weighting. It occurs randomly and is expected to cancel out. The result is: the equally weighted index beats the market-cap weighted index by 1.5% to 2%. This improvement in return may seem insignificant but it is not. Look at Table 5 below.

In resume, the improvement by 1.5% to 2% is a vindication of our observation market-capitalization weighting is intrinsically defective because it reinforces the distortion that Mr. Market injects into the stock prices. The equal weighting is independent of prices and thus is neutral to the price distortion by Mr. Market. As we suspected, it results in a significant improvement in portfolio returns.

How can we improve the equally weighting procedure? What about giving weight according to a measure of economic size to the companies? We go to the next section.

8.4 Fundamentally Weighted Index

Fundamentally Weighted Index - Table 4

Company B = $300 million / $1 billion = 30% weight in index

Company C = $200 million / $1 billion = 20% weight in index

Company A = $100 million / $1 billion = 10% weight in index

Company D = $400 million / $1 billion = 40% weight in index

For the fundamentally weighted index, we used earnings as a measure of economic size. Earnings for the entire universe of companies equaled $1 billion, so Company B, with $300 million in earnings, receives a weight of 30% in this fundamentally weighted index. Fundamentally weighted indexes often use additional measures of fundamental size such as cash flow, book value, sales, and/or dividends. Notice that market capitalization (and therefore market price) is not considered in this fundamental index.

In the fundamentally weighted index, we use the sales, the earnings, the book value, or any measure of economic size. In Table 4, we used earnings as listed in Table 1 above.

Just like for the equally weighted index, we expect overall that the over-weighting of unduly bid up stocks and the under-weighting of unduly bid down stocks, still occur but not systematically, arising from the very procedure, as is the case with market-cap weighting. It occurs randomly and is expected to cancel out. The result is: the fundamentally weighted index beats the equally weighted index by less than 1%.

Summary

In resume, the fundamental weighting using a measure of economic size such as earnings, is independent of prices and thus is expected to perform better than the market cap weighting. Weighting using economic size reflects the performance of the economy and thus is expected to perform better compared to equal weighting. The two weighting schemes, so far discussed, although they yield improvement over the market cap weighting, are neutral with respect to the "margin of safety" principle.

On the other hand, value weighting directly invokes the "margin of safety" principle in its procedure. The procedure buys only unduly bid down stocks of good companies, and no unduly bid up stocks! Thus, we expect the value-weighted index to perform way better than the other three schemes. We will see that we will not be disappointed.

Below is a comparison of the returns of the four weighting schemes.

(a) The first is S&P 500 index Total Return (this is market-cap weighted index), giving average 20 year CAGR of 9.1%;

(b) S&P 500 Equal Weights, 11.8%;

(c) FTSE RAFI 1000 Index (fundamentally weighted index), 12.2%; and

(d) Value Weighted Index, 16.1%.

To see the implications of these CAGR to your nest egg starting with $5,000, see Table 5 below.

Table 5: Comparison of Returns

5,000				
No Years	9.10%	11.80%	12.20%	16.10%
5	7,728	8,733	8,891	10,547
10	11,946	15,254	15,809	22,248
15	18,465	26,644	28,110	46,930
20	28,541	46,538	49,984	98,995
25	44,115	81,286	88,877	208,822
30	68,189	141,979	158,036	440,491
35	105,399	247,989	281,009	929,175
40	162,915	433,154	499,671	1,960,012
45	251,816	756,574	888,482	4,134,470
50	389,231	1,321,479	1,579,839	8,721,295

Value-weighted index will be a topic in the next chapter—9: Greenblatt Investing Approach. We will examine the basis for the value weighted index in terms of the Greenblatt investing approach.

Chapter 9: Greenblatt Investing Approach

In this chapter, we want to understand why the value-weighted approach to index investing as defined by Joel Greenblatt yields superior returns compared with the rest. The approach is a contemporary embodiment of the two perennial pillars of sound investing. One pillar is due to Benjamin Graham, universally considered the "the father of stock investing": the "margin of safety" or "pay a lot less", made possible by Mr. Market offering unduly bid down stocks.

The other pillar is due to Warren Buffett, the most successful stock investor and a student and business partner of Benjamin Graham: to buy companies at below average prices is good; but to buy good companies at below average prices is even better. Let's see how Joel Greenblatt combines these two perennial pillars of sound investing in his value-weighted approach.

9.1 Earnings yield

To be able to compare apples to apples in selecting stocks, we need a suitable quantity. We cannot just use the price of a stock. The price in itself does not indicate the value of a share of stock. Combining price with earnings, the key entity for a company, by dividing the price by earnings, P/E, the so-called Price Earnings Multiple, we get a quantity that is comparable across stocks.

Remember, the value of a company is the sum total of the stream of earnings over its lifetime properly discounted to account for the time value of money. A stock which costs $20 per share, with earnings of $5, has a P/E = 4. Another stock priced at $15 per share, with earnings of $1, has a P/E = 15. From these examples, we see that the lower price of $15 is not necessarily the cheaper stock, because you are paying $15 per dollar earned. Compared to the other stock at price $20, this is cheaper because you are paying only $4 per dollar earned.

To see this differently, we take the inverse of P/E, i.e. E/P, or what is the so-called Earnings Yield. This presents a wholly different psychological view of the situation. We now see the ratio in terms of the idea of a "return" on what you paid for— the yield of the money you put in. Going back to our examples, the first stock has a P/E of 4, and inverting the ratio, gives an earnings yield of 0.25 or 25%. The second stock has a P/E of 15, giving an earnings yield of 6.67%. If you were asked to choose a stock, obviously you will choose the one with the higher earnings yield.

With the concept of earnings yield, you can compare the yield of the different stocks you are considering, as well as compare the yield of the stocks you are considering with the interest (or the yield) given by banks for time deposit, or the interest that a bond will give. Suddenly, you have a way of comparing the different investment opportunities at hand. And with the idea of "pay a lot less" or the "margin of safety", you will choose the investment that gives the higher yield, because the price multiple is low, or what is the same, because the earnings yield is high.

Earnings Yield Ranking

So, the upshot of the whole discussion above, boils down to this: to implement the "pay a lot less" or "margin of safety", you would purchase stocks with a high earnings yield or with low price multiples. So, imagine a whole universe of stocks. At any time, some stocks are unduly bid down because of Mr. Market's fear, and some stocks are unduly bid up because of Mr. Market's greed. If you list all the stocks, from 1 to 3,500, say, according to their earnings yield from the highest yield to the lowest, you have a list with which you can implement the "pay a lot less" or "margin of safety" principle of sound investing. Depending on the amount of money you have to invest, you will decide where you cut the list. But, before we do that, we have almost forgotten the other pillar of sound investing—the idea of Buffett.

9.2 Return on invested Capital

What if instead of ranking the companies according to earnings yield, we also rank them according to how "good" the companies are. The quality "good" is captured by the Return on Invested Capital. Say, you have an ice cream company. Your total investment is $50,000. Your profit is $5,000 a year. Your Return on Invested Capital (ROIC) is 5,000 / 50,000 = 10%.

On the other hand, your brother is running a shoe company with a total investment of $50,000 but has a yearly profit of $10,000. This translates into an ROIC of 20%. If you were asked to choose between the two companies, obviously you will choose the shoe company because it is the better company than the ice cream company.

So, we have another important consideration to take into account when we rank the companies to choose for our investment. Suppose, we rank the same universe of companies, from 1 to 3,500, according to "goodness", i.e. according to their return on invested capital, from the highest to the lowest return. Now, we have a list from where we can select the "good" companies and it is not necessarily the case that the list is identical with the list of "earnings yield".

The question: how do we combine the two rankings? By simply adding the rankings in both lists.

9.3 Combined Ranking

Say, a stock is 150 in the "earnings yield" list and 271 in the "returns" list. The combined ranking is 421. Another stock, say, is 1 in earnings yield list but is 3,500 in the returns list. Its combined ranking is 3,501. The combined ranking gives a list of stocks which embodies a compromise of the two important traits--high earnings yield or low price multiple, and high returns on capital.

Another way to put this, the combined ranking does not select stocks with high earnings yield but with low return on capital; nor select stocks with high return on capital but with low earnings yield. It selects stocks with both relatively high earnings yield and relatively high return on capital. Still another way of saying this, the combined ranking selects above average companies at below average prices.

In resume, the combined ranking of "earnings yield" and return on invested capital embodies the two perennial principles of sound investing: (1) the margin of safety principle or "pay a lot less" principle and (2) the Warren Buffett principle—to buy companies at below average prices is good; but, to buy good companies at below average prices is even better.

It is clear that an approach to investing that uses the combined rankings is the way to "load" the dice in your favor. What do back-studies actually show on the performance of an investing approach that uses the combined rankings?

9.4 Magic formula investing

Let us examine the result when we apply the formula of the combined ranking, which Greenblatt amusingly calls the Magic Formula, from the back-testing study he conducted covering the years from 1988 to 2004. The result, using the combined ranking, where he chose only from the top 30 stocks in the list and held the stocks for one year and repeated the procedure every year from 1988 to 2004, is just spectacular!

Essentially, the investing approach of Prof Joel Greenblatt consists of the following steps: (1) from the combined rankings, choose 24-30 stocks from the top 30 in the list to populate the portfolio. Stagger the purchase of stocks over the course of the year—about 4 to 5 stocks every 2 months; (2) keep the stocks for one year: the losers you sell a few days before one year is up and the winners you sell a few days after one year is up—for tax purposes; (3) replace the sold stocks choosing from the top 30 in the combined ranking list.

The one year period, as I understand the approach, is a compromise between selling early less than a year and selling after more than a year, given the distribution of times when a fair value is attained in a portfolio of 24 to 30 stocks. Different stocks are like different kinds of fruits. They ripen at different lengths of time. Instead of figuring out the "ripening" time of each stock—which may involve emotions—the approach cuts through the "guesswork" with a statistical knife: harvest when one year is up.

The compound annual rate of growth of money invested, using the combined ranking of Joel Greenblatt, over the 17 years from 1988 to 2004 is 30.8%!!! That is just INCREDIBLE! Your money of $11,000, for the same years would have ballooned to $1,056,147! More than a million! The return of 30.8% beats the record of Warren Buffett of 29%.

The result from the back-testing studies is without explicitly determining the value of the business of each company represented by the stock!!! That in itself is incredible! *The combined ranking circumvents the difficulty and the hard work needed to determine the values of businesses.*

This is what I mean when I say the Greenblatt method is equivalent to valuing a company without doing it! The details of the Greenblatt approach are found in his book, "The Little Book that Still Beats the Market".

Since the publication of Greenblatt's book in 2005, where he revealed the combined ranking method in picking stocks, which he jokingly called "magic formula investing", the public in general has not taken notice of his approach. He has appeared in conferences, on TV talking about the combined ranking approach. Among those who know it, few have stuck to the approach.

If the returns are that spectacular, why is the public not beating a path to its door? It is our old friend—our emotion dependent short time horizon and other "biases", the topic in Part 1. Let us see why.

Why Magic Formula Will Continue to Work

If an investing approach becomes widely used, then the approach will lose its edge. The reason is the great majority of investors will buy the stocks selected by the approach and thus the prices of the said stocks will immediately reflect the information. In other words, the information is quickly discounted in the prices. If the magic formula becomes widely used, then its "magic" will cease to work. But, all indications point to a bright prognosis: it will continue to work because humans are too "human". Let me explain.

The returns of the magic formula are lumpy, as we expect. Over one-year rolling periods from 1988 to 2004, on average, its return underperformed the overall market five months out twelve. On average over four-year rolling periods, its return was worse than the overall market once every four years. For every six-year rolling periods, its return was worse that the market for more than two years in a row. In the seventeen-year periods tested, its return underperformed the market for three years in a row.

Do you think it is easy to stick with the magic formula when it hasn't worked for years in a row? Many will take it for a curiosity ride for a few months or a few years. But, the great majority will abandon the formula when it underperforms the market, or when they hear that their friends have better returns. Humans have a very short investment time horizon and, as shown experimentally by Daniel Kahneman, are very poor intuitive statisticians.

Indeed, humans do not understand and appreciate the statistical nature of the 17-year average compounded return of 30.8%! By the nature of stock investment returns, that long-term result of 30.8% is an average—it comes in lumps. When the lump is negative and big, investors ran away because of the pain they are suffering now.

In a way, that is the good news! We are lucky that the magic formula does not work all the time! If it works all the time, then everybody uses the formula, then the prices of the stocks selected by the formula would immediately go up and thus, there would be no longer any bargains—no more opportunity to "pay a lot less" or for a "margin of safety". [This fact, in effect, shows that in the stock market those who know profit from those who know not or are simply ignorant].

Those whose brains can overcome the emotions of the moment giving rise to short time horizon; those whose brains can ignore the pain in the short term and see the gain in the long term; those whose brains can appreciate the long time nature of investment returns; those whose brains can think in terms of probability and see the statistical nature of portfolio returns—will benefit from the magic formula of Greenblatt. And they are few—those who read this book may belong among the few.

Greenblatt's approach to index investing is based on this powerful result. To finish off this "magic formula investing", I will give the results of the updated version: from 1988 to 2009, including the big market crash in 2007 to 2009.

Corresponding to the result of 30.8% is the result of 23.8%. The result is still spectacular given the huge crash of the stock market in 2007-2009. It is almost 3 times the return of the overall market as represented by the S&P 500: 9.5%.

In his website, www.magicformulainvesting.com, Greenblatt publishes every day, the top 30 stocks selected by the combined ranking of all the stocks traded in the US exchanges with a market capitalization of over 50 million dollars. This comes to choosing only the 30 top ranked stocks out of about 3,500 stocks—the 30 cheaper but good companies, whose prices are unduly bid down for some reasons. So far, it is for free.

9.5 Value-Weighted Mutual Fund

Unfortunately, you may not have the requisite funds yet to invest the magic formula way. Your funds may yet be small. To my mind, the minimum to start investing using the magic formula is $50,000. You need to buy about 24-30 stocks over the course of a year—selected from the top in the combined rankings. The next best thing is available to you: the mutual fund that uses the Greenblatt approach of combined ranking based on earnings yield and return on capital—whenever it will be available.

[Note: In the Preface, I indicated that my son opened an account in a mutual fund managed by Greenblatt and his associates. But, sometime May 2014, they seem to close the mutual funds and transferred the accounts of clients to Gotham funds. The minimum amount required is now $250,000.]

You may study other value-weighted mutual funds. Definitely, the initial amount needed is smaller than $50,000— about $5,000 to open an account in a mutual fund. When your fund becomes $50,000 or more, then you may opt to switch to investing the magic formula way.

Summary

It is anticipated that investment firms will move toward value-weighted indexes in the near future. You open an account, plunk your $5,000 in or whatever is the amount and forget it, until you retire. You can see what to expect from your $5,000 from the Table below.

The value-weighted funds are expected to be top performers. We expect this because its very scheme directly invokes the two perennial pillars of sound investing: (1) the Graham principle of "margin of safety" and (2) the Buffett principle of "buying good businesses at below average prices". The two principles may be combined and stated thus: BUY ABOVE AVERAGE COMPANIES AT BELOW AVERAGE PRICES.

Nest Egg

This is all about your nest egg: money you set aside for your retirement; that you put in an investment, that in time will become BIG enough for you to live comfortably in your golden years. The question you ask: what investment vehicle? I assume not all of you want to pick stocks. With that assumption, my simple answer is: a value-weighted mutual fund.

9.6 Is it possible to waste three precious years?

In section 6.3, we saw the long time horizon of investment returns: as the time horizon increases, the probability of losing money decreases to zero; and the probability of a higher return increases. It is a mathematical property of exponential growth that the longer it is operating, the faster it accelerates. The ideal holding time for stock investment is 30, 40, 50 years—which is the usual length of time till retirement. And if you do not have the time to do investing properly, or no inclination to pick stocks, then mutual fund is for you.

If you have the inclination to manage a stock portfolio, then the Greenblatt approach to investing is for you—the magic formula investing: https://www.magicformulainvesting.com/.

Is it possible that we could waste three precious years if the Greenblatt approach will be found wanting? I hope at this point you are convinced that it will not be so. The choice of stocks is based on two principles that underpin sound investing, principles that stood the test of time. One is the Graham principle of "margin of safety"; and two, the Buffett principle of "buying good companies at below average prices".

Prof Joel Greenblatt started a hedge fund, Gotham Capital in 1985. By definition, only high net-worth individuals who invest in millions are allowed by law to invest money in hedge funds. Knowing that he has been very successful in his investment firm, his relatives and friends were asking him "how to invest" for the small investors.

For a long time, he admits that he did have a good answer. He was anxious to help the small investor, like his relatives and friends. Finally, he wrote a book meant for the small investor, "The Little Book That Beats the Market" in 2005. He followed with another book for the small investor, "The Big Secret for the Small Investor".

With these two books, in particular the second book, he is satisfied that he can finally declare that he has answered the needs for the small investor. But, like I said in the section on "Why Magic Formula Will Continue to Work", only those who really understand the long term nature of the time horizon of investment returns will benefit from the Greenblatt approach.

May your golden years be financially comfortable!

Table: Comparison of Returns

5,000				
No Years	**9.10%**	**11.80%**	**12.20%**	**16.10%**
5	7,728	8,733	8,891	10,547
10	11,946	15,254	15,809	22,248
15	18,465	26,644	28,110	46,930
20	28,541	46,538	49,984	98,995
25	44,115	81,286	88,877	208,822
30	68,189	141,979	158,036	440,491
35	105,399	247,989	281,009	929,175
40	162,915	433,154	499,671	1,960,012
45	251,816	756,574	888,482	4,134,470
50	389,231	1,321,479	1,579,839	8,721,295

Part 3: IQ in support of EQ—An Investing Approach

We know from modern psychology that our EQ leads all our decision-making. We can overcome the biases of our EQ by acquiring new information, which our EQ can draw upon in making decisions. The acquisition of new information is the main activity of our IQ.

The central idea that underpins everything—choice of investing approach, overcoming of our weaknesses, taming of our emotions, management of our portfolio—is the simple *two-component model of portfolio return.* The model captures the two essential component behaviors of portfolio return—the statistical and the "drift" or causal exponential component.

Portfolio return is the reason why we invest in the first place. An intuitive understanding of its behavior over time helps us make better decisions. Otherwise, we are just investing blind. We will continuously be perplexed by its seeming inscrutable ways. We will constantly be whipsawed between euphoria and despair.

To my mind, understanding the two-component model of portfolio return is key. Stock investing is like trapping an elusive quarry. Without a clear idea of the characteristics of the quarry—like how it looks, what its size is, how quick it is—we will come back from the hunt surely empty handed.

To hold our heads while others are losing theirs, it is crucial that we have an intuitive grasp of the long-term dynamics of portfolio returns. The understanding of the two-component model by our IQ will be a source from which our EQ can draw upon to guide our emotions and consequently our actions.

I repeat our EQ leads our decision making. Our EQ needs all the accurate information about the "quarry" for making correct decisions. Our EQ needs all the support that our IQ can provide.

Chapter 10: The Arrow and the Hoisting Crane

In this chapter, we gather together all the key elements, dimensions, properties, characteristics on stock returns—the two-component model we developed, scattered in previous chapters and sections—in one place.

10.1 Stock returns: a composite picture

Return variability with time

Stock returns behave differently depending on the time scale. Daily returns exhibit the highest variability. Twenty-year returns, on the other hand, show very low variability. For time scales in between is a continuous spread—from that exhibited by daily returns, to that shown by twenty-year returns.

As our time scale increases, the probability of losing money decreases to zero: what I call the "law of long times". The natural time scale for returns is in decades.

Stock return is like a current in a wire

In chapter 2, we compared a stock return to a current in a wire. An electron, a constituent of a current, undergoes random motion due to heat. But, at the same time, superimposed on its random motion is a "drift" velocity due to a "drift" force in a given direction.

Likewise, portfolio return consists of moving stock prices. A stock price undergoes random up and down motion due to the random buy and sell by millions of investors. But, superimposed on the random motion of prices is an upward exponential "drift" arising from the net buy over the long term—more buys than sells—and the fact of compounded growth. As we argued in section 6.2, there are more optimistic investors than pessimistic ones.

Stock return is like a drunkard walking

In section 6.2, we also compared a portfolio return to a drunkard's walk. At every step, a coin is flipped: heads, drunkard moves forward; tails, backward. The forward step is longer than the backward step; its length increases with time. The backward step is constant in length. The net buy over the long term corresponds to the difference in length of forward and backward step. The increasing forward step with time represents the compounded growth rate.

If we let the drunkard walk for a long time, then we find the drunkard is at some distance away from his start. If we plot the distance along the y-axis; the time along the x-axis—then we get a wiggly curve which goes up and down; but, overall has an upward drift or trend.

Money growing like a microscopic fertilized egg to you

In chapter 1, we compared the compounded growth to a cell undergoing division. With some simplification, when we do the calculation, we come to the conclusion it takes just 45 cell divisions to transform a microscopic fertilized egg to a full-blown human with 37.2 trillion cells. Likewise, a small amount of money can balloon to a huge amount in 40-45 years of compounded growth.

To complement the cell division analogy, in section 6.2 we also presented the notion of compounded growth as a process similar to the prodigious growth of a rabbit population.

Money growing like a rabbit population

The essence of a rabbit population growth is that babies give birth to other babies: that a quantity—number of rabbits—grows in proportion to itself: initial number + gain in number. A repeat of the cycle in only a finite number of times produces a colossal number—what may be called an EXPLOSIVE growth.

In a portfolio return, the initial amount + gains in the first year are rolled forward in the second year. The amount at start of second year + gains are again rolled forward in the third year and so on.

This growing of "something + growth" proportional to itself is what is known in finance as compounded growth; in ordinary talk, as explosive growth; and in mathematics, as exponential growth. This is essentially the same process going on in our portfolio returns—if rolled forward, the gains will generate other gains.

Share prices depend on supply and demand

Ultimately, share prices—the constituents of returns—depend on supply and demand. In the short term, the supply of shares is constant. It takes years to create new supply of shares. It starts with a company contemplating to go public in what is called an IPO, initial public offering. There are steps to follow and requirements to meet before approval for an IPO is given. Also it takes years to decrease the supply of shares by company buybacks and mergers.

What about the demand? The psychology of investors shapes the short-term component; while the fundamentals of the Economy drive the long-term component of the demand. The psychological disposition of investors explains the short-term volatility of share prices—consequently, the short-term volatility of returns. Investors who act based on the fundamentals of the Economy, as well as those investors attuned to the supply side, explain the long-term trend of share prices—and thus, of returns.

Summary

In summary, our portfolio return has a random component. Think of an electron that moves forward and backward along a wire with random probability due to heat. Or, think of a drunkard who steps forward or backward according to a coin flip. From these images, we see our return change value back and forth, positive and negative due to buy and sell by investors.

However, superposed on the random motion of the electron is a "drift" velocity due to an external applied force or voltage. Likewise, at the same time that share prices randomly move up and down, they also drift upward at compounded growth.

10.2 The arrow and the hoisting crane

How shall we picture all these composite elements? To build an image, we should realize at its base everything about portfolio returns all boils down to **sentiments**—how investors feel about the shares of stocks.

Imagine an arrow with its pivot attached to a rope hung from a hoisting crane. The arrow rotates about its pivot. The hoisting crane slowly lifts or lowers the pivot, by winding or unwinding the rope in slow motion, as the whole device moves to the right with time.

That is the make-up of our **sentiment device**. We call it **the arrow and the hoisting crane.**

The arrow rotates to point up or down at every buy or sell. Its length is proportional to the net change in prices or the net change in the value of our portfolio. It rotates like crazy—as many millions of times as the number of buys or sells daily. The arrow has a built-in intelligence that computes the residual—the net change in share price, either positive or negative, added to our portfolio daily.

The residual is passed on to the hoisting crane. Note the residual computed takes into account the compounding growth effect. Essentially, compounding comes from the fact that we roll forward the total amount—the original + the gains. We buy shares using the total amount. So, when the arrow computes the residual, it takes account of all shares bought by the initial amount plus all the gains at a point in time. At the end of a trading day, the arrow either points up or down, with length proportional to the residual.

We can set the time scale by which our hoisting crane operates—daily, weekly, monthly, yearly; or in decades. It has a built-in intelligence that sums the residuals passed on by the arrow at all scales and the corresponding average compounded annualized growth rate, the CAGR, over the time period. The hoisting crane hoists the pivot up or down according to the residual at the set time scale. The crane moves the pivot to the right in sync with time.

So, a typical scene is the following. Remember, the natural scale for returns is in decades. Since the hoisting crane represents the "drift" exponential component—the return, we set it in decades. The arrow is set to its natural time scale—in seconds.

On any trading day, we witness the arrow furiously rotating—to point up, or, to point down. But, the pivot hardly moves at all. The hoisting motion of the crane is the drift motion—it represents our return. The slow, if majestic motion of the hoisting crane, tells us it is foolish to act on the time scale of the arrow. This is the image we should have of our return—the snail-paced motion of the hoisting crane representing the "drift" component; and the squirrel-hurry motion of the arrow corresponding to the random component which sums up to zero.

In effect, we have separated the random component from the causal or drift component of the return. The random component cancels out to zero—the arrow simply rotates about the stationary pivot. The causal or the drift component is what constitutes our return.

Thus, the motion of the pivot traces the total value of our portfolio according to the time scale we set.

We can think of our sentiment device this way: the madly rotating arrow of variable-length represents the short-term sentiments—the random component of returns—changes in share prices which largely cancel out, leaving a residual which could be positive or negative; the slow lifting or lowering of the pivot by the hoisting crane corresponds to the long-term sentiments—the causal or "drift" exponential component of returns—the sum of the residuals over a long time.

The long term sentiment is ever present; it is most of the time positive. But, more or less at regular intervals, the positive sentiment builds up over a long time to a peak. Then, for some reason, the positive sentiment turns negative in a relatively short time. Our hoisting crane unwinds the tether furiously, sending the pivot in a free fall. Upon reaching its lowest point, the crane usually jerks the pivot up by a quick winding of the rope. And so goes the story of the stock market boom and bust.

10.3 Transfers of wealth from the poor to the rich

What do all these mean in terms of people? In terms of you or me? What I have just described are the **great transfers of wealth in bear markets,** from those who do not have much to those who already have so much! Remember, for every seller, there is a buyer. So, in a massive sell-off when an ordinary investor who does not know much about the nature of the stock market and therefore vulnerable to fear and greed, envy and herd mentality—sells his shares at great discount of his purchase price, he is selling to someone in the other side of the transaction who knows much about the stock market and who has tons and tons of money just waiting for such an opportunity.

To put it crudely, but rather accurately—a bear market is a massive transfer of wealth from the poor to the rich! The recent example is the 2007-2009 bear market!

They say, great wealth changes hands in a bear market. But whose hands—from whose hand to whose hand?

Just a thought: if everybody holds on to his/her stocks, there will be no massive sell-off and thus no massive transfer of wealth!

This is the pipe dream of this book!

10.4 CAGR—a way to view our stock investment

There are many ways we can view anything. The same is true with investing in the stock market. If we look at stock investing using a short-term lens, we see distorted optics—the distortion comes from randomness. As we saw in chapter 2, we are not wired to handle this distortion. Yet, most of us, due to our lack of knowledge of the nature of returns, make decisions based on this distorted view.

To clear the fog covering our view, we look at stock investing using a very long-term lens: in terms of the average annual growth rate over a long period—CAGR "lens", compound annualized growth rate.

Let us take the example of the US stock market. The standard benchmark for returns for investors in the US stock market is the S&P 500 index. In Table 1, we have the index return from 1988 to 2004. At the end of Table 1, we see the CAGR is 12.40%. This means over the whole period of 17 years, from 1988 to 2004, in each of these years, we can think the US stock market returns 12.40%. We can regard this as the "effective" annual growth rate over the 17-year period— averaging the lumpiness of the returns, ranging from +37.6% to -22.1%.

From this "average growth rate" lens, every portfolio over a long period of time has its CAGR. Now, the name of the game is to beat the S&P 500 index CAGR, which historically is about 10-12%. Our concern is to beat the 10-12% average compound annual growth rate of the S&P 500 index.

You cannot beat the 10-12% CAGR by responding to the "antics" of the arrow; or, by anything having to do with fluctuations. The arrow, standing for randomness, does not add anything to the CAGR of your portfolio. In fact, anything you do in response to the arrow actually degrades your return—and not enhances it, contrary to your intent.

What could we do to improve the CAGR of our portfolio? The choice of investing approach is the first key action. If you plan to invest in a mutual fund or ETF, from our discussion in chapter 8 and 9, investing in market capitalization weighted index funds is the same as shooting yourself in the foot. Most index funds are market cap-weighted.

We saw in chapter 9, value weighted index funds perform much better than all other funds. The reason is their very construction—these funds do not systematically overweigh unduly bid up stocks; nor under-weigh unduly bid down stocks. In fact, these funds consist of unduly bid down stocks.

So, the weighting of the stocks in the funds' portfolios is crucial in its effect on the CAGR.

The whole idea is this: you want to populate your portfolio with stocks attracting a higher demand due to the fact their prices are below fair value—the lower, the greater is the demand.

In resume, the hoisting crane computes the CAGR over a long period. Its motion could be calibrated to show the return curve at a given CAGR. The CAGR-calibrated motion can only be influenced by the net buy over the period; the net buy in turn depends on the demand by investors; the demand by investors depends on how far below their fair value are the prices of stocks in the portfolio.

We will see the systematic way by which the Greenblatt approach goes about finding the "cheap" and "good" stocks by his combined ranking method, in the next chapter.

Chapter 11: Which Investing Approach?

"The underlying principles of sound investment should not alter from decade to decade, but the application of these principles must be adapted to significant changes in the financial mechanisms and climate."

Benjamin Graham

Now, the question: which investing approach do we choose? To answer this question, we use our understanding of the two-component dynamics of stock returns—the arrow and the hoisting crane.

11.1 Using the arrow and the hoisting crane

I myself meandered in the space of investing approaches. I started with the Warren Buffett approach of buy and hold, without the acumen of Buffett in the choice of stocks or the company underlying the stock. I did not meet with success with the buy and hold approach due to "poor" selection of stocks. From hindsight, a key factor for the buy and hold strategy is the quality of stocks chosen. No matter how long you hold a stock—if it is a lemon—it remains a lemon all the hold time. What a cost in opportunity.

Riding the second level part of the drift force

Given the nature of stock returns, what is the investing approach that best rides the "drift" force? In considering this question, we focus our attention on the hoisting motion of the crane and not on the rotation of the arrow. We know two levels of the causal or drift forces drive the motion of the hoisting crane.

How shall we ride best the second level part of the drift force: the compounding growth of the net buy? We consider this question first because the answer is straight forward. The investing approach must stipulate a long holding time to fully harness the rabbit-like growth of the net buy. Together with the requirement of safety of capital, the holding time must be at least 20 years. This result we established from a statistical analysis of stock returns in chapter 6. As we enunciated in the "law of long times", as the holding time increases, the probability of losing money decreases to zero.

11.2 Riding the first level part of the drift force

Principle of margin of safety

How should we ride best the first level part of the "drift" force—the net buy over the long term? This is where the two perennial principles of sound investing come in: Benjamin Graham's principle of *margin of safety* and Warren Buffett's principle of *buying good companies at below average prices.*

If we buy companies with a margin of safety, i.e. at a price lower than their fair value—paying a lot less—on average, statistically speaking, the number of net buys and the amount of each net buy are greater than when we buy shares at or above its fair or intrinsic value.

Remember the net buy over the long term is what sets the motion of the hoisting crane.

There is greater demand on stocks perceived to be priced below their fair value. This is the mechanism by which the prices of said stocks rise. It may take time for other investors to see the situation as a bargain.

We assume that eventually investors will agree the stocks we pick populating our portfolio are below their fair value, irrespective of whether they represent ordinary or good companies. On average, many are likely to buy and in greater number of shares. How long shall we wait for other investors to agree with us? We take a statistical compromise—we hold our stock for one year, as we saw in section 9.4.

Furthermore, if we buy good companies at below average prices, then, on average, the same result above is statistically expected: the number of net buys and the amount of each net buy are greater compared to the case of buying at or above their intrinsic or fair value—even more so, compared with the previous case. Now, we have good companies, instead of just ordinary companies, at prices below their fair value.

The demand for the stocks is even greater for the case of good companies than the case of ordinary companies.

Mr. Market supplies unduly bid down stocks

How do opportunities like those above arise? Why do prices of companies go down below their fair value, thereby enabling us to apply the *first principle* of sound investing: the *"margin of safety"* principle? Using Mr. Market as a metaphor for the psychology of investors, Graham points out there are always stocks that are unduly bid up, as well as unduly bid down.

How so? When a company misses analysts' earnings estimate, which to begin with is at best questionable, investors' reaction tend to be exaggerated. With our bias to loss aversion, as well as to fear, we tend to overreact to bad news. Investors who hold shares of the said company may dump their shares sending the price unduly down, much worse than what the fundamentals of the company underlying the stock truly reflect.

On the other hand, when a company for some reason receives much favorable attention from the press, and/or hyped reports, such as Microsoft in the making; or the next Apple; or the company is run extremely well, etc.—with our bias to believe and to greed, many of us form an exaggerated regard for the said company. We look at the company in much better light than what its fundamentals are saying. In our list of choices, we find ourselves ranking the said company as our first pick. Many of us will buy shares of the said company bidding the price unduly up.

Where does this lead us? To the conclusion, at any time: (1) there are unduly bid down stocks, arising from our biases of fear and aversion to loss; (2) there are unduly bid up stocks, due to our biases to believe exaggerated reports and to greed; and (3) we have to develop a method of finding out especially the unduly bid down stocks.

If we can find a systematic way of discovering the unduly bid down stocks, then we can comply with the first principle— the margin of safety, or, paying a lot less. This means we will only have in our portfolio unduly bid down stocks. We are paying for them a lot less. We have a margin of safety.

But, wait. Is it the case an unduly bid down stock or a cheap stock is always undeserving of its low price? Or, is it the case that many low-priced stocks deserve the sentiment with which investors regard them?

Principle: buying good companies at below average prices

Caveat emptor! Beware buyer! Many cheap stocks are cheap because they deserve it. This brings us to the **second principle** of sound investing from Warren Buffett. He remarked: buying companies at below average prices is good; but, *buying good companies at below average prices is even better.*

So the algorithm for our search is: look for unduly bid down stocks and choose the good companies among them; or, equally, look for good companies and choose only the unduly bid down stocks among them. This is the search formula for stocks by which we will populate our portfolio.

At this point, we are settled on the conceptual criteria for our choice of stocks/companies—cheap and good. We believe our criteria of cheap and good, i.e. good companies bought below fair value, enable us to optimally "ride" the first level part of the drift force, thereby optimizing our returns—sending the hoisting motion of the crane up the most.

To put it differently, buy good companies lower than their fair value. And sell them when they hit their fair value.

We now have to translate the concept of "cheap" and the concept of "good" into quantitative properties for convenient comparison to facilitate our search.

11.3 Greenblatt approach to stock investing

This is the point where the various approaches differ—the operationalization of the two principles of sound investing. One management group uses as many as 19 variables. Here, we follow Greenblatt who uses only two variables: (1) earnings yield; and (2) return on invested capital.

Earnings yield

In chapter 9, we saw the price of a share of stock by itself is not an indication of its cheapness. It is the ratio of price to earnings, P/E, or PE that indicates the relative standing of a stock to other stocks in regard to its cheapness. Data is available for this variable, P/E. To facilitate our thinking to see the ratio in an intuitively revealing way, we invert the ratio into E/P, the so-called earnings yield—which means the earnings or interest we get from the price we pay for a share. This way of looking at the PE ratio makes it easy to compare different asset classes, like the yield from CD, or the bond yield.

Moving to the practical, we can use a computer to rank stocks according to earnings yield: the higher the earnings yield or the cheaper the stock, the higher the ranking. It is possible to rank all stocks in an exchange with respect to earnings yield.

Return on invested capital

What is the corresponding quantitative property that measures "good" companies? We saw in chapter 9, a yardstick that spells the viability of a company is ROIC—return on invested capital. A hen that does not lay eggs is as good as dead. Similarly, a company that produces low returns will not last long. The company with high ROIC will kill its competitors.

Again, we use a computer to generate a ranking of the same companies we rank with respect to earnings yield, now with respect to ROIC: the higher the ROIC, the higher the ranking.

Combined ranking

The earnings yield ranking is not the same as the returns-on-capital ranking. How do we combine them? A way to combine them is to simply add the rankings in the two lists. Say, there are 3,500 companies. Say, company A has a ranking of 1 in earnings yield—it is the cheapest; but, a ranking of 3,500 in returns. So, its final rank is 3,501. Company B has a ranking of 21 in earnings yield; but, a ranking of 100 in returns. Thus, its final ranking is 121.

Using the Greenblatt approach to investing, we will populate our portfolio with 24-30 stocks chosen from the combined ranking of earnings yield and return on invested capital.

Summary

In terms of the arrow and the hoisting crane, the Greenblatt approach to investing optimally rides the drift force, thereby maximizing the CAGR of the portfolio, i.e. by causing the hoisting motion of the crane up the most.

We may say the combined ranking of earnings yield and return on invested capital generates what I call "Goldilocks" stocks—neither too hot, nor too cold; or too high in earnings yield, nor too high in returns on invested capital—but, just right. In the words of Joel Greenblatt, we populate our portfolio with stocks of above average companies at below average prices.

We expect from the 24-30 stocks in our portfolio, on average, a greater net buy compared to other approaches. Statistically, we expect a greater demand for the "Goldilocks" stocks in our portfolio. This means a greater CAGR of our portfolio return; in turn, a greater displacement up of the hoisting motion of the crane.

Chapter 12: Re-programming our mind

"The best-laid plans of mice and men often go awry".

Adapted from Robert Burns

With the choice of investing approach settled, we now consider the issue of how best to execute it. Our Emotion or EQ, we know from modern psychology, orchestrates all our decision-making. Our Emotion could heed the whispers from our Reason; it could equally overrule our Reason.

A good part of stock investing is spending time to educate our Emotion, our EQ. An action done once has a passing effect. However, an action repeated many times becomes a habit. To overcome our "biases", we have to cultivate tendencies that become automatic. We do the cultivation by repetition. In effect, we use repetition to establish ready-to-use modules our EQ can use to act contrary to our "biases".

12.1 Ready-to-use modules by EQ

Say, the stock market is in a free fall. After the initial shock of disbelief, you start calling your friends. One by one, you receive the answer you are prepared to hear—yes they have sold or are selling their stocks. An inner voice tells you that you will lose a lot of money if you do as your friends are doing.

However, Evolution prepared us for fight or flight. This module—the fight or flight response—resides in our brain, ever ready to use. Similar packages are resident in our brain, which our Emotion can use anytime without much thought. In this instance, you ignore the voice of reason and choose the ready-to-use flight response.

To relate my own personal experience, I have thought a lot about the behavior of the stock market. I know, for example, that the alternation of "red" and "green" in my portfolio is just a result of random events. Despite knowing a "red" is just a statistical fluctuation, even now I still have a niggling feeling the negative return is permanent, accompanied by a fleeting fear. If the day after, it is still red, my niggling feeling is reinforced.

I realize the depth of the sculpting of the traits we inherit from our ancestors in the savannahs in Africa.

On the other hand, I do not do crazy things due to the alternating "red" and "green" in my portfolio. My understanding of the nature of stock returns is able to restrain my emotions. This understanding my emotion draws upon to guide my action.

Re-programming our mind is the use of repetition of images and/or statements silently to our minds until the actions arising from them become automatic—a process I call educating our Emotion. This is the focus of this chapter.

A diagnosis without a corresponding treatment or cure is worse than useless. It makes known the disease; however, this knowledge is dis-empowering since you cannot do anything to affect the course of the said disease. It is like someone undergoing a genetic test where the result shows she has the gene of an incurable disease.

We are at a point where we know the diagnosis of our "biases"; the weaknesses of our nature. On the other hand, we now have an understanding of the nature of portfolio returns. What can we do with this knowledge? We can use our knowledge of the nature of returns and the diagnosis of our biases to re-program our minds.

12.2 The arrow and the hoisting crane

The central metaphor encapsulating the key ideas in this book is **the arrow and the hoisting crane.** It is a metaphor of **our portfolio return.** The motion of the arrow represents the random component; the hoisting motion of the crane, the causal or drift component. The ramifications of the image have the potential to nullify all our biases operative in stock market investing.

The arrow, if down, rotates about its pivot to point up for each buy; if up, rotates to point down for each sell. Its length varies in proportion to the change in price or the change in portfolio value. Daily, the arrow sums the total buys and sells into a net amount or residual. Depending on whether the residual is positive or negative, the arrow either points up or down at the end of a trading day. If the residual is expressed in percentages, we get the daily returns in our portfolio. If put side by side, the arrows look similar to Figure 1.

The motion of the arrow represents the random component of returns: it sums up to zero.

The pivot attached to a rope is hung from a hoisting crane, slowly lifting or lowering the pivot by winding or unwinding the rope in slow motion, as the whole device moves to the right, in time. The arrow daily passes on the residual it computes to the hoisting crane. The natural time scale of the hoisting crane is in decades—in contrast, the arrow's natural time scale is in seconds. The crane processes the daily residual passed on by the arrow into amounts proper to weeks, months, years, and decades. We set our hoisting crane to its natural time scale in decades: the x-axis—the time axis—has marks 1, 2, 3, 4, 5, etc. corresponding to decade 1, decade 2, decade 3, and so on.

The hoisting motion of the crane represents the drift component of portfolio return—it sums up to the total gains or profit over the period, arising from a net buy over the long term.

So, let's go through a typical scenario. It is trading day at the start of January. We switch on our sentiment device according to their natural time scales: the arrow in seconds and the hoisting crane in decades.

Right at the opening bell of the stock exchanges, the arrow is furiously rotating about its pivot—pointing up, pointing down, as many times as there are buys and sells. And there are millions of them; at different times, at various amounts. Throughout the course of the day, we hear the erratic whirr of the rotating arrow.

Yet, in the midst of the frenetic activity of the arrow, the hoisting motion of the crane is hardly perceptible at all—up or down. There is no perceptible motion in a day; in a week; in a month. In a year, we perceive a small motion.

This is our problem: the stark contrast between the rotating motion of the arrow and the hoisting motion of the crane—the wide gap in time scale; the incommensurability of time horizons; the mismatch between our emotional time and the investment time horizon.

12.3 Overcoming our biases

Short time horizon

The nature of the "drift" force is such it takes decades to show results, with the requirement of safety of capital. As we saw in section 12.2, the hoisting motion of the crane representing the "drift" force is naturally slow, with a time scale in decades.

The mantra I suggest to overcome our tendency to view things with a short time horizon and expect quick results is: *"the natural time scale for returns is not days, but decades"*. To go with the statement is the image of *the snail-paced winding up or winding down of the rope by the hoisting crane.* We conjure up the image and say the statement to ourselves silently whenever we are aware of our impatience; or, otherwise, wanting a shortcut to wealth.

Poor intuitive statistician

The nature of the random force is captured by the motion of the arrow. The fact returns flip between positive to negative values is not important. The flip is just random. The purely random part of our return just cancels out to zero, represented by the arrow staying put at its pivot—no matter how fast or how many times it rotates. Yet, for many of us, our attention is focused on the alternation of "red" and "green" in our portfolio.

What we should focus on is the cumulative positive amount arising from the "drift" force—the net buys over the long term. This is what gives us the return; not the random component which eventually cancels out to zero.

The mantra I suggest whenever you are tempted to do something to your portfolio when you see "red": *"the drift component gives us the return; not the random component". Or, the snail-paced hoisting motion of the crane traces the curve of our return; the squirrel-hurry rotation of the arrow adds nothing to our return.*

Loss aversion

We saw in chapter 3, loss aversion prods us to prematurely sell our winners and unduly keep our losers. As we will show in the next chapter—13, with the Greenblatt approach I recommend and follow, we keep our stocks for one year. For tax purposes, we sell our losers a few days before one year ends; while we sell our winners a few days after one year ends.

If you adopt the Greenblatt approach and follow the guidelines, loss aversion is not a problem. Besides with our understanding of the two-component model of returns—the arrow and the hoisting crane—we are no longer bothered by anything that randomness can throw at us in connection with our returns. They are just the "antics" of the arrow.

Envy and herd mentality

In chapter 4, we saw the source of our envy is a result of chance or randomness. Our friend's return happens by chance to be higher than our return. This is allowed for by randomness. Now, with our grasp of "the arrow and the hoisting crane" metaphor, we realize envy of returns of others resulting in our imitating others' portfolios is foolish. Our focus should be the "drift" component and not the random component.

Herd mentality arises when an investor does not have an explicit investing approach. The investing approach I follow and I recommend is the magic formula investing. One of its guidelines is to stay invested at all times. The phenomenon of the herd mentality is especially notorious at bear markets—it is partly the cause of it. With our conviction that the investing approach we are following is sound, then we are not susceptible to the herd mentality.

Fear and Greed

In chapter 5, we saw fear and greed as two sources of opportunities in the stock market. At special times, the two are the sources of great transfers of wealth—from those who do not have much, to those who already have too much.

To put it crudely but rather accurately, fear and greed are the causes of great transfers of wealth, *from the poor to the rich.*

We are susceptible to the emotions of fear and greed if we do not have an explicit investing approach. In chapter 11, we discussed an investing approach which satisfies the nature of stock returns, as well as the two perennial principles of sound stock investing.

Anyone who has an explicit investing approach and who understands the nature of stock returns—yet succumbs to fear and joins the mass sell-off is a living contradiction.

Anyone who has an explicit investing approach and who understands the nature of stock returns—yet yields to greed at the height of a bull run when valuations are bloated, and loads up on stocks as they see others doing the same—is a living contradiction.

12.4 EQ and IQ working together

To be able to hold on to our investing approach and not abandon it when under pressure, we have to understand the rationale behind the investing approach we have chosen—be it the Warren Buffett approach, or Phil Town approach, or the Ken Fischer approach, or the Greenblatt approach (I highly recommend), or whatever. When the going gets rough, when our expectation does not match the portfolio reality, the only anchor we can hold on—is our understanding of the chosen investing approach. Nothing else will do.

That is our EQ depends on our IQ. Our understanding of our investment approach helps us restrain our emotions. This is what I mean that a successful investor needs both IQ and EQ—they are complementary.

Summary

A key to re-programming our mind to overcome our biases to become better stock investors is to accept **our Emotion leads our faculties in all our decisions.** Modern cognitive psychology, in the pioneering work of Daniel Kahneman and Amos Tversky, finds that we behave as if two systems operate in our mind, labeled System 1 and System 2 by Daniel Kahneman.

System 1 is thinking fast, automatic, effortless and emotional. System 2 is thinking slow, deliberate, effortful and logical. System 1 plays the lead role; System 2, the support role.

For short, we may call System 1—Emotion; while System 2—Reason. For sound bite, we may call System 1—EQ; while System 2—IQ.

With that as a background, a step to overcome our biases is to be aware of our biases and observe our tendency to do exactly as the bias is described. Part 1 is aimed at sensitizing our awareness to our biases relevant in stock investing. The next step is acquiring information on the nature or the reality of the stock market. Our emotion can draw upon the information as a basis for alternative actions other than those to which our biases lead us to. The goal of Part 2 is precisely the enhancement of our understanding of the nature of the stock market. This chapter—12 brings the diagnosis of our biases and our grasp of the nature of the stock market into the re-programming of our mind to become a better stock investor.

Chapter 13: Managing our portfolio

In this chapter, I assume you are investing for a long time—at least 20 years; better still, forever. When we say you invest for twenty years, we mean as your money grows you keep rolling it forward invested in stocks. Of course, if your money has grown substantially before the end of 20 years, you can withdraw some or all of it.

You may have extra money which you do not need to defray your living expenses; or money you do not need within 20 years or so. You may be a college graduate with a job, just like my three sons. Aside from work related retirement account, one of my sons opened his own personal retirement plan in a stock mutual fund, where he makes a quarterly deposit.

I have been investing in stocks for 17 years. I started as a mutual fund investor in June 1998, opening an account in Vanguard. I slowly build up an understanding of the confusing and confused world of stock investing. When I felt confident I know enough not to "throw" away our hard-earned money, my wife agreed: I manage our account online. We opened an account in discountbroker.com in January 2001. Eventually, TD Ameritrade acquired the company. We closed our account in Vanguard and transfer the funds in our personal account in discountbroker.com.

13.1 Standing toe-to-toe with two grizzlies

I never look back since then. I certainly made my share of mistakes. The mistakes were mainly in the choice of stocks. I was overconfident in my ability to pick stocks. A number of the companies were lemons. And one was found to be fraudulent. But, with opened eyes I bought shares from those companies.

What Warren Buffett means

One thing I learned early on is not to bail out during a bear market. I learned to stay invested when everyone else seemed to push the panic button. I held on tight as the stock market nose-dived to -22.1% in 2002. Having survived the bear at the start of the decade, I took advantage of the 2007-2009 market crash toward the end of the decade. It was, then, I fully realized what the famous remark by Warren Buffett means: *be fearful when others are greedy; and greedy when others are fearful.*

What Daniel Kahneman means

It has drastically changed my thinking about myself, about humans. We are not what we think we are. We are *emotional animal, prone to error; but open to correction with the use of our reason.* This view is completely different from the prevailing view among the educated. This view is different from the dominant view in the Social Sciences and the Humanities.

I clearly saw, then, the zero-sum-ness in the stock market. Those who understand the statistical nature of stock returns, thereby are able to hold their emotions, get the positive sum. Those who do not, get the negative sum.

Game of zero-sum-ness

Why do I say so? In the stock market, for every seller, there is a buyer. The unfortunate investor who follows the herd in a massive sell-off is selling shares 30%, 40%, 50%, 60% off his buying price—he loses big time. The investor on the other side of the transaction buys at a huge discount who stands to gain what the other loses and possibly more. Invariably, the stock market recovers and reaches a peak higher than before the crash. That is the game of zero-sum-ness in the stock market.

My new definitions of bear and bull market

As a result of my experience in the 2007-2009 market crash, I have my own definition of a bear and a bull market. In the common definition, a bear market is one where the stock market is down greater than 20%.

In my definition, a bear market is a great transfer of wealth, from those who do not have much, to those who already have too much. In cruder terms, but rather more accurately, a bear market is a great transfer of wealth, from the poor to the rich. Probably, the 2007-2009 bear market was the greatest wealth transfer ever.

In the common definition, a bull market is one of overall rise in share prices. In my definition, a bull market is one long preparation for the great transfer of wealth, which follows immediately at the end of the Bull Run.

We can view the same situation from another angle—the Matthew effect. Those who do not have the requisite IQ and EQ, even that which they do not have much shall be taken away. This exacerbates the gap between the haves and the have-nots.

It is one of my motivations in writing this book—not only to benefit my three sons; but to anybody who is interested. This is my contribution to even the playing field.

I was able to convince my wife—not an easy task—we load up on stocks in 2009. And we did. Some of my buys were right at the bottom of the bear market when there was a massive sell-off on March 2009. This once-in-a-lifetime opportunity compensated for the effects of my previous mistakes and some.

Maintenance Procedures

Based on the investment approach we have chosen, we populated our portfolio with stocks. How do we manage our portfolio?

For those investing in a mutual fund, the maintenance is simple: (1) make additional deposits as your finances allow; and (2) stay fully invested at all times even during a bear market.

For those investing in an individual account, there are maintenance procedures we have to keep. To be specific, although commonalities exist regardless of the investing approach adopted, nevertheless for the sake of clarity I assume you are adopting the Greenblatt magic formula for investing. See chapter 9 and chapter 11.

13.2 Staying put when a bear comes

I am not talking here of a real bear, in which case we run for our lives. I am talking about a bear market. Instead of selling all, we buy all we can afford to buy in accord with the guidance of our chosen investing approach. It may seem counter intuitive to buy when a massive sell-off is going on. If we think about it, the huge sucking pressure brings down prices in its train—the good companies, as well as the bad ones. We still have to be choosy, though, according to the guidelines of our investing approach.

There are few individuals who can time the coming of the bear. I have read all the books by Ken Fisher—the son of the legendary Phillip Fisher—a successful investor in his own right, who manages a multi-billion fund for his clients, who claims in his book, "The Only Three Questions that Count"—he was able to sneak a peek at the bear as it was preparing to launch its devastating carnage in three of the last four crashes. The last one, the 2007-2009 market crash, he failed to read the signature. For as he relates in his book, the signature for each is different. If you have the time and the patience to study the previous footprints of the bear, though they will not be directly useful in future sightings, they could help you figure what the new signature could be.

But, for us ordinary investors, we have a simple and very potent defense against a marauding bear. Ignore it. Just keep going. Do you want to hand in your hard-earned money to the already rich many times over, who is just waiting for you to hand in your money to his grasping hands? This is exactly what you are actually doing when you join the herd in the massive sell-off during a bear market. Keep your money with you by staying put.

Ask yourself this question: why would anyone buy when you sell during a mass sell-off? Remember you cannot sell your shares if there are no buyers. Because the buyer knows you are selling your shares dirt cheap and therefore exorbitant profits when surely as night follows day the stock market recovers, nay even reaches a peak higher than before the crash.

Put yourself in the shoes of a buyer, in the mindset of a buyer during a market crash. The stock market is the Amazon store of stocks. Sales at huge discount everywhere you look. In this situation, would you rather be a seller, competing with others giving away huge discounts; or would you rather be a buyer, where the choice of quality shares of stock is dizzyingly huge?

Let us do ourselves a favor. Let's not hand in our hard-earned money to the already very rich—filthy rich.

Having stood toe to toe with two grizzlies, a smaller one in 2002, and a colossal one in 2007-2009—I learned it is possible to overcome the primal emotions of fear and greed, sculpted deep in our psyche. I was not worried the recovery will take time. I did not need the money invested in stocks in the near term. I know the stock market will recover. I was focused on buying quality stocks, than engaging in fear of the end of the world economy.

13.3 Staying invested when a bear comes at retirement

If a bear comes at or near the time of your retirement, then it poses some problem if you did not adequately prepare for it. The question on what to do when a market crash occurs when you retire, assumes you properly plan your retirement, aside from the work-related retirement account. This means you opened a retirement account at least 40 years or so ago. Some 6-7 years before retirement, you should insure you have funds in CDs and/or savings account enough to pay for all your living expenditures over a period of about 5 years. By this time, your personal retirement account (different from work-related retirement account) is substantial. You may trim it to fill any shortfall to your 5-year living expenses emergency fund. You maintain this 5-year living emergency fund in a CD/savings account as long as you live, with the bulk of your money invested in stocks. If and when a market crash occurs when you retire, you do not panic; you do not bailout. You stay fully invested. You can live on your emergency fund.

13.4 Leaving a core investment

When you retire at age 60, or 65, or 70—you may still have 30, or 25, or 20 more years to live. It is not as if at retirement, you withdraw all your money and close your account. No, at retirement, you begin to withdraw money from your retirement account, at set intervals, say every quarter, where you judiciously sell shares of stocks in the quarter before you use the fund. You have a window of 90 days to time your sale when the market is up. If you did your retirement plan right, you will have a core investment fund which continues to grow even as you trim it for living expenses. You may even have something to leave for your grandchildren.

13.5 Maintaining your portfolio

Portfolio maintenance in magic formula investing is straight forward. Having populated your portfolio with about 24-30 stocks selected from the top 30 in the combined rankings, over the course of a year, buying four or five stocks every two months—you leave them alone for a year. For tax purposes, you sell your losers a few days before one year is up; while the winners you sell a few days after one year is up. You replace the sold stocks with new ones selected from the top 30 in the combined rankings of earnings yield and return on capital.

The buying of stocks is staggered over the whole year. You keep the stocks for one year. Your selling, then, is also staggered over the whole year. You go through the same process—year in and year out. It is that simple.

Summary

There are three key actions we have to do to manage our portfolio. One, we follow the guidelines of our chosen investing approach in populating our portfolio with stocks. Two, we keep invested all the time—come what may—a bull market, a bear market, a recession or a depression. Three, we prepare for a bear market by keeping in a CD or savings account an emergency fund for living expenditures good for five years, for as long as we are alive.

Conclusion: IQ and EQ

Once again, we revisit the issues on IQ and EQ. In the end, it is through our understanding using our IQ we acquire new information which our EQ can tap as a new basis for action. This is what I call educating our emotion.

We acknowledge our EQ leads our decision-making. IQ plays the support role. Our Emotion could rule out our Reason and take action based on a package we call instinct—as when we dump our shares in a bear market out of fear.

Here, we close our discussion on stock investing by answering the question as to the minimum level of IQ and of EQ to succeed in the stock market.

Minimum IQ for a successful stock investor

The level of intelligence—IQ—required in the stock market is the ability to understand: (a) the rationale behind an investment approach in terms of two principles: (1) Benjamin Graham's margin of safety—availing of Mr. Market's buying-selling opportunity; (2) Warren Buffett's buy criterion—buying good companies at below average prices; and (b) the statistical nature of stock returns.

If you understand an investment approach in terms of the two principles above, as well as the statistical nature of stock returns, then you pass the required level of intelligence, the minimum IQ hurdle, for a successful stock investing.

This understanding of the investment approach you choose is crucial in reining in your emotions from blowing up into madness, as we saw in Part 1 and 3.

Minimum EQ for a successful stock investor

Here comes the difficult part—***our Emotion, our EQ. O****ur Emotion plays the lead role in all our decision-making, including those in stock investing.* Our Reason plays the support role. Emotion is the source of opportunities, when coming from others; at the same time, of losses when coming from us.

Now, what is the level of—EQ—emotional intelligence required to be successful in stock market investing? It is the level of EQ that enables us to stick to our chosen investment approach, no matter what happens in the stock market. If the stock market soars, we don't buy more shares/stocks than our approach stipulates. Likewise, if the stock market crashes, like the horrendous crash in 2007-2009, we don't dump our shares/stocks. We maintain equanimity   and continue to execute as our investment approach tells you to execute.

That looks easy enough to do. But, when the rubber meets the road and you have a significant skin in the game, all manner of reasons to abandon your chosen investing approach for a seemingly better one bedevil your mind. When you see everybody else is buying or selling, you begin to have doubts about the correctness of your approach. When your significant other nags you that stocks are inherently "unsecure", you begin to waver in sticking to your approach, especially when there is a significant drop in the value of your portfolio.

If you can hold the "urge" to follow the herd and buy shares because everyone you know is buying, then, you pass the level of emotional intelligence, the minimum EQ hurdle, for a successful stock investing. If you cannot, then stock market investing is not a way for you to make money.

It is in the nature of stock returns that they exhibit statistical fluctuations. Say, your portfolio is a few percentage points behind the S&P 500 index. Or, your portfolio, compared to your friend's portfolio, yields a lower return. If you let your emotions guide your actions, then you are likely to abandon your investment approach and change to one tracking the S&P 500 index, or to one like your friend's.

If you can hold the "urge" to change approach just because your portfolio lags behind others, then, you have the requisite emotional intelligence, the minimum EQ, for a successful stock investing. If you cannot, then stock investing is not a way for you to make money.

If you succumb to the temptation to abandon your approach, you will be engaged in chasing the "hot" index or the "hot" mutual fund; or the "hot" portfolio among your friends. "Heat" chasing is not a viable investing approach.

Emotion pushes us to investment mistakes

We have so much difficulty adhering to a well-thought approach, even a winning investment approach, because our emotion induces us to do something—anything—as we see "red" numbers in our portfolio due to statistical fluctuations in the returns, or, for any reason for that matter.

A study showed that mutual fund investors on average hold on to their portfolio only 3.2 years. Their returns average 3.2% compared to the benchmark with a return of 8.2%—a full 5% lag. That is a huge underperformance over the long term. They invest in and out at the wrong time. Failing to grasp the statistical nature of stock returns, we make too frequent changes in our portfolio, achieving the opposite of our intent—reduced returns.

Our Emotion could short-circuit our Reason. It does this often, most especially in the absence of ready-stored understanding of a situation. EQ usually does not wait for lazy Reason to find things out before EQ acts. When EQ goes straight to action without the input from IQ, it succeeds most of the time. Sometimes it succeeds spectacularly. At other times fails miserably!

A market crash is the most strenuous test your EQ could be subjected to, like the recent crash in 2007-2009. It needs all the support your IQ can give. From Reason, a market crash is supposed to be the best time to load up on stocks, add positions as much as your money allows, as much as your approach allows. This statement may seem counter intuitive. Come to think of it, a big drop in stock prices means that many good companies are extremely cheap. They are on fire sale! The stock market went on sale at unprecedentedly low prices in 2009 crash! Coupled with the fact that the price you pay determines the return you get, market crash is the best time to load on stocks.

However, our Emotion with an inherited ready-to-use-model of fight or flight may short-circuit our lazy Reason and decide to fall on the default action: to flee the stock market. So, instead of loading up on stocks, as our Reason would have found out if it tried, we dump our shares/stocks. We suffer the Newtonian madness. This is the madness which Newton spoke of in his outburst: "I can calculate the motion of heavenly bodies but not the madness of people". This is part of the madness, in its many manifestations, that stands in the way to making money in the stock market.

Our "biases" lead us to "madness"

The weaknesses of human nature, or our "biases" show unmistakably in a big way during stock market crashes or bubbles. The behavior of people during a bubble cannot be described in any way, except as pure madness. In the run-up to the bubble, people pile up to get a share of a seemingly priceless security, pushing the prices sky-high; then, as surely as night follows day, out of nowhere, they find themselves holding a worthless security and dump their shares almost for nothing.

No other actions show more "madness" than this. A madman can do no better!

A smaller "madness" plays daily in the stock market, as when someone abandons an investment approach to switch to one like her friend's, just because the return of her portfolio lags behind her friend's. Or, when someone buys or sells just because everyone else is doing so.

Antidotes for madness

In the 5 chapters of Part 1 and especially in chapter 12, re-programming our mind, we presented antidotes for this madness! By following the argument in this book, rehearsing it in your mind like a mantra, you would have taken a step towards inoculating yourself from Newtonian madness where it matters most—in the stock market.

Many think they can easily pass the IQ hurdle. And I wholeheartedly agree. Equally, many think they can easily pass the EQ hurdle because they are rational. However, from what we know about the losses from bubbles in the past and the losses from the recent 2007-2009 crash, I respectfully disagree.

From what we know of human nature, the "biases" we are born with, operating in our minds below the conscious level, predispose us to "madness" that may lead to a permanent loss of our investment capital. If you are unaware of the weaknesses of human nature; if you do not reprogram your mind to overcome these weaknesses, then you will not pass the level of EQ for a successful stock market investing.

You may have the IQ, but not the EQ!

Mantra and images

Whenever you think about anything related to the stock market, to stock investing—I suggest you think of the arrow and the hoisting crane. The rotating motion of the arrow stands for the random part of stock market returns. The random part is a mask—it is the "face" we see daily in our portfolio. The mask hides the real return. We strip the mask for what it really is—

just random and sums up to zero, adding nothing to our return. It is appropriately represented by an arrow rotating to point up or down but stuck to its pivot—it goes nowhere.

The hoisting motion of the crane, on the other hand, stands for the causal or "drift" part of stock returns. The drift part is actually the return; but it is difficult to see due to masking by the random part in the short term, as well as its slow build-up in decades, not in years. The yearly net buys sum up to the total gain over a long period. The hoisting crane winds up the rope faster, the longer the time. Or, the gain grows like rabbits; or like we grow by cell division—from a microscopic fertilized egg to a full human in just 45 cell divisions.

I suggest we repeat these like a mantra:

"The actual return is masked by randomness";

"The actual return is shown by hoisting snail-paced motion of the crane"

"The natural time scale of returns is in decades, not in years".

The law of long times: "As the holding time of our investment increases, the probability of losing money decreases to zero".

With images and statements like those above—we can formulate more—we will slowly educate our emotions to making the right investing decisions.

Parting thoughts

Investing in the stock market is a way of making our money work hard for us. In my case, the idea took a serious turn when I no longer could work for money due to my Parkinson's illness. I have to earn my keep to defray my medical expenses.

To stay alive in the best possible "way" is a strong motivation to dig as deeply as I can into the "essence" of stock investing.

To my mind, the "essence" of stock investing is captured by the arrow and the hoisting crane—a metaphor of our experience with the stock market, in particular with stock returns. The motion of the arrow is what we directly see and experience daily—the alternating "red" and "green" of our returns. The arrow is the source of grief and investing mistakes for many of us. The arrow is the focus of our emotional response. We should learn to ignore it because its motion adds up to zero return—much ado about nothing.

On the other hand, the hoisting motion of the crane we do not directly see or experience. The natural time scale of the hoisting motion of the crane is in decades. Over a time period, the return of any portfolio has a specific CAGR. The period in consideration is long enough in decades to insure a positive return. The CAGR-calibrated hoisting motion of the crane is smooth, tracing the curve of our return, starting the upward motion slowly at first and picking up acceleration the longer the time. We should learn to focus our attention on the hoisting crane precisely because the hoisting motion of the crane is our return.

In chapter 11, we used the hoisting crane to "explain" why or how the two perennial principles of stock investing work—paying a lot less or the margin of safety and buying good companies at below average prices. The net buy over a long period sets the hoist into motion. This is the mechanism of the hoisting motion of the crane. In effect, the two principles populate our portfolio with stocks with prices below their fair value. Consequently, investors seeking bargains will buy shares of stocks in our portfolio, thus raising their prices. On average, the net buy is greater, compared to the case of a portfolio populated with stocks with prices at or above fair value.

Seeing the CAGR-calibrated motion of the hoisting crane is many steps removed from our day-to-day thinking. Training our mind to see it is to educate our Emotion on a new basis for action. Once the image is internalized, then the following attitude of mind becomes automatic: we naturally ignore the arrow altogether. It is like leaving the ocean surface in a hurricane and diving down into depths where the waters are calm and still for peace and quiet.

Consequently, our Emotion, which orchestrates our decision-making, is calm, executing our investing approach, from the viewpoint of decades, knowingly ignoring the short-term fluctuations. Firefighting in response to the arrow becomes irrelevant.

Re-programming our mind along the lines above, via repetition, transforms what we know, what we learn into modules our Emotion can call at any instant.

Our IQ's grasp of the arrow and the hoisting crane will serve as a ready-to-use module our EQ can call in making investing decisions, in precise consonance with the title of this book, *"IQ plus EQ: The Arrow and the Hoisting Crane"*.

Appendix: questions my son asked

My son had some questions which add to a more solid understanding of aspects of stock investment. I specifically call your attention to question 1 and the answer. It deals with the issue of a market crash, where declines greater than 20%, 50% or more occur—how to prepare for a market crash, what to do during a market crash, and how to manage your portfolio.

Question 1:

So it seems that in the long run, you will always gain money if you invest in stocks? Is that a correct understanding? So regardless of the short-term fluctuations, is what the studies have found that the overall trend of the stock market is that you will always gain money in the long run?

Answer 1:

That is a correct understanding—provided you do not withdraw your money at the wrong time. Let's take a specific example. Let's say you invested $5,000 and held it for 50 years. By January 2008, your money has ballooned to $2,000,000. You had 2 million in your account and by October 26, 2008 you would be in retirement. You know the stock market crashed in 2007-2009. Your retirement coincided with the worst stock market decline since 1929.

What a horror!!! By October 26, 2008, your nest egg lost $600,000 and continued to hemorrhage at an alarming rate. By March 2009, your 2 million would have been reduced to 1 million. If you were like many investors, you would have bailed out and sold everything. At what point you would bail out would depend at what point you no longer could take the massive hemorrhaging of your money. At any point, you would have lost a substantial portion of your retirement money. At the lowest point, you would have lost 1 million of accumulated money. Trillions of dollars were lost worldwide by the "poor" during the

2007-2009 stock market crash—*because people bailed out instead of doing nothing during the crash.* But, the same trillions went to the already super-rich! It was a scary time to be in stocks. And our herd mentality would sweep us into the wrong action, if we did not prepare our minds beforehand.

What should you have done? Do nothing during the crash. Do nothing? When you stood to lose your remaining million from March 2009 on-wards? By the way, nobody can tell whether the stock market is at the bottom of the crash or not. Yes, that's right. Do nothing. It is as certain as night follows day that the stock market will recover in three to five years. The stock market recovered to the level of Jan 2008 at 1400 by about March 2012, a little over four years. Your money would have returned to two million in a little over four years.

But you were ready to retire by the middle of the crash, you protest. How do you reconcile your retirement and "doing nothing" during the crash? You expected to start withdrawing money from your account on a regular basis during retirement. Here is the way. Six to seven years before your retirement, you should insure you have an emergency fund for living expenses for 5 years—money deposited in a CD or savings account. This fund could partly come from your personal retirement in a mutual fund or individual account. In chapter 13, we indicated the desirability of opening a personal retirement account separate from the work-related retirement account. If you followed the suggestion in this book, you would have opened this account 40 years or so ago. Near the time of your retirement, money in the account could be substantial allowing you to trim some amount for your emergency fund.

So when October 26, 2008 came, you had ample provisions for your everyday needs for 5 years in liquid assets, like bank CD or savings to tide you over for the period of a stock market crash and thus, you can "*do nothing*" during a crash. Note 3 years after your retirement, October 26, 2011, the stock market has substantially recovered about 77% of its value before the crash.

This means your money has gone up from the low of 1 million to about $1,540,000.00. Though your portfolio has not fully recovered yet, if pressed you could start withdrawing for your monthly needs by selling shares and keep the rest invested so that your money continued to grow until the end of your life. Remember, you may still live many more years—decades even—during your retirement. So you want your money to grow to be able to keep pace with your expenditures in your retirement. As the stock market continues to recover, you sell shares periodically to keep in CD or savings account money enough for 5 years provisioning in case another crash comes. You continue to manage your portfolio in this way.

Follow-up to Question 1:

But I still want to ask, what is the mechanism or the "thing" that makes you so sure that in the long run, the stock market is always on an upward spiral? Is it just speaking from experience of what happened in the past? So we're just going by empirical evidence of the long run trends in the past and assume that they will continue to be like that in the future? (with fluctuations of course). Or, is there some other mechanism that I'm missing that governs the stock market saying that in the long run, the stock market is always increasing and if you wait long enough, any loss you make will come back to you.

Answer to Follow-up to Question 1:

The basic mechanism of why the stock market, in the long run, is always on an upward spiral is this: in the long run the economy is always spiraling upward. The economy of the US and other countries too always expands in the long run, allowing for temporary contractions during a recession or a depression. Remember the stock market is a leading indicator of the economy, i.e. it swings up ahead of the economy (about 6 months or so) and hits bottom well before the economy in a recession hits its lowest point. So, your question transforms into: why does the economy of a country always expand or grow in the long run? Because the goods and services grow to keep pace with the growth of the population. For as long as there are people demanding more goods and services, there will be companies producing those goods and services, and thus the economy inevitably grows. The long-term growth of the economy means the long-term growth of the stock market. Remember the stock market is a mechanism by which companies finance their enterprises. Buying a share of the stock of a company, is a way to participate in the growth of the company and in the growth of the overall economy.

The overall long-term behavior of the British economy, for example, from 1100 to 1995 is a flattish curve until the steep rise in real per capita income after the onset of the Industrial Revolution in 1750 in the United Kingdom. The Industrial Revolution is a turning point in the history of the world. It spread to Europe, North America, and Asia. Humans in a large way realized that they can be more productive by harnessing the mechanisms of nature that they understand with Science and therefore can exploit through Technology. The industrial revolution still is continuing, but it no longer is the leading edge in growing the productivity of workers. The next wave of productivity enhancing revolution came with the widespread use of computers. The current wave of productivity enhancing revolution is upon us—the real-time connectivity via the internet, both stationary and mobile. Each wave raises the relative peaks of productivity ever higher, thus resulting in the ever upward spiraling of the economy, and the parallel ever upward spiraling of the stock market.

The same phenomenon is shown in the upward rising long-term real growth in US GDP per capita from 1871 to 2009; as well as the long-term growth of the US stock market.

Question 2:

Also, me being paranoid, when you give your money to these mutual funds (like Greenblatt's for example), what stops them from cheating you out of your money? I guess I'm speaking in the context of what happened with Madoff. I'm not sure of the details in that. But it seemed a lot of people lost money because they trusted him with their money. Just like I would be trusting Greenblatt's mutual fund. Sorry if that sounds ignorant. I'm not actually sure how these things work yet.

Answer 2:

What is a tell-tale indicator that a stock investment firm is involved in a shadowy deal or a scam? The tell-tale indicator is that the stock investment firm *guaranties a constant return year in and year out without fluctuations.* In the case of Madoff, the guaranteed constant return was 10% - 12%.

What human characteristics make us easy prey to this type of scam, even those who are supposed to know better? Two characteristics: *greed and loss aversion.* These two traits, together with a lack of real understanding of the relationship between return fluctuations and the investment time horizon, make for a dangerous brew that makes humans easy prey for these kinds of scams.

By and large, 99.9% of investment firms in the US are safe. They are highly regulated by the US Government. But one or two escape detection. Greenblatt has been running an investment firm for 30 years now. I guarantee his is not a scam.

Question 3:

This raises another question for me. Which is: if this mechanism is so sure, and the stock market always increases, why doesn't everyone have this insight that you should just keep your stocks and '*do nothing*' as you said if there is a recession or a down turn in the stock market. Wouldn't it be logical that everyone knows this if this is such a big underlying principle? Or are most people so short-sighted and impatient to follow this even if they know it?

Answer 3:

The simple answer is that the vast majority of investors and would be investors do not know this. And even if some know it (intellectually), the vast majority of those who intellectually know it cannot execute it. This goes back to the subject matter in Part 1 on the "biases" of human nature: we humans are not adapted to stock investing. We still have the brains and instincts of our ancestors in the savannahs in Africa. We do not think in statistical terms. We are poor intuitive statisticians.

Do you think it is easy to hold on to "big underlying principle" when everyone—your brothers and sisters, your friends and acquaintances, strangers—has jumped the ship into the cold waters? Do you think it is easy to hold on to "big underlying principle" when your friends whisper to your ears that it is time to jump ship?

You begin to doubt the big underlying principle, as you continue to see others plunging into the sea. You begin to entertain the thought that "perhaps there is a good reason why they are jumping into the waters". When you are all alone on the deck of the ship, it takes tons of courage and a strong gut feel that everybody who jumped ship is wrong and even though you are alone that you are right. This all too human herd mentality takes over the vast majority of investors who intellectually know the big underlying principle--but their emotional gut feel says otherwise. You will see what I mean when you have a skin in the game.

Those who have executed according to the big underlying principle are super rich and they are few.

You have to realize that the investing world is awash with advises, advisers, claims and counter-claims of successful approaches, hucksters selling their services, pundits who pontificate about their sure-fire methods, charlatans who pass as experts, books, and tapes—all sorts of sources of information, disinformation and misinformation. I have seen it all. If you are a beginning investor, you will be lost in a babble of confusing claims of the best approach to investing. Your assumption that it is logical to expect that everyone knows the big underlying principle is simply not true, given the treacherous paths you have to navigate to obtain the correct information. In the first place, if you are a novice, then you are not in a position to know which is true, partly true, or totally false.

Thus to obtain the correct information is almost a random event. There is a price to pay to obtain the right information in terms of time, effort, rejecting what you later found to be wanting or patently false, and adjusting to insights that are helpful from others and from yourself.

The information, which I believe is correct information, I am sharing with the three of you, is hard-earned. I spent a good portion of the last decade studying what investing is all about, the essence of the stock market, the underlying principles that stood the test of time--in at least 25 investment books of the serious kind that I have accumulated over a decade. The books and thoughts of the masters in investing, such as Benjamin Graham, Warren Buffett, Philip Fisher, Joel Greenblatt, including the Nobel-prize winning Daniel Kahneman on Behavioral Finance (the behavior of humans detrimental to stock investing) etc., I have studied and absorbed. I spent a year running computer simulations to see for myself the long-run trends of the stock market and my runs confirmed that the longer the time period, the less the fluctuation and the less the risk. I have put to action what I learned and adjusted to new insights.

How many of the investors, and would be investors, take the time and the resources and the seriousness to study the essence of investing, just as I did? I'm afraid, not many. That's why not everyone has this insight on the big underlying principle.

Question 4:

My new question is: is the cycle of crashing and recovering always 3 to 5 years? Can it ever be over 10 or 20 years? So for instance hypothetically. Let's say I am 70 years old when there is a crash. It continues to crash. I do nothing. Five years have gone by, and still the stock market is decreasing and I'm losing lots of money. I still do nothing. Ten years have gone by. Still it is decreasing I am losing even more money. I have almost no money now. But yet I hold firm and do nothing. Fifteen years go by and still the same thing. And then 20 years have gone by I have almost nothing, and was living in poverty for the last 5 years of my life. And then I die at age 90.

And then suddenly after 20 years, the market picks up again and stock markets increase and my investments eventually come back up again and my money returns to the level it started with when I was 70 years old and even surpasses it. But by this time it is of no use because I am now dead, and even spent the last years of my life destitute. Whereas if I had pulled out of the stocks within the first few years of the crash, I might have been able to live more comfortably in the last 20 years of my life. Is there any basis for this argument? Or do markets always recover within 3 to 5 years just like in your example that you gave with the market crash of 2008?

Answer 4:

Now your question: is the cycle of crashing and recovering always 3 to 5 years? Then you proceeded to describe a scary scenario where the stock market continues to decline for 20 years! Is this scenario possible? We have to remind ourselves that the space of possibilities is infinitely huger than the space of probabilities.

The scenario you described is certainly possible. But it is not probable. Would you hold back an investment in stocks on the grounds that the US economy will collapse on Monday? By doing so, you are investing on possibilities. Remember that investing in stocks is a probabilities game, and not a possibilities game. That the US economy will collapse on Monday is highly improbable, approaching zero probability.

My specific answer to your question, the only reasonable approach to it, is to look at the historical record for a rough estimate of the probability of occurrence of your scenario.

Access the graph of the US stock market, as represented by the S&P 500 index, from 1929 to 2011 in http://www.ritholtz.com/blog/wp-content/uploads/2011/10/chart.png. It indicates the periods of recession (in dark bands) and the bear market periods—the turning points indicated by big dark dots. We see that the worst bear market coincided with the Great Depression of 1929, where the stock market plunged -86% in the mid-year of 1932. During this 82-year history, there is no occurrence at all of a 20-year decline in the US stock market. At the worst, the decline was 3-4 years, and recovered partially within 3-4 years after the onset of decline; or recovered completely.

So, though your scenario is possible, it is highly improbable based on the historical record that I have. You can examine each decline in the stock market and get a sense of the time of the actual decline and the time from the onset of decline to partial recovery or total recovery. If you count, there are 17 bear markets in the 82-year period. Thus, on average, you have a bear market (a decline of 20% or more) every 5 years. Some bears are near the minimum. A few bears are huge, like the 1929-33 crash, as well as the recent 2007-2009 crash.

So my take home idea, is that investing is a probabilities game and not a possibilities game. The odds are the stock market partially recovers or recovers completely or hit a higher relative peak in 3-4 years from the onset of the bear market.

About the Author

Feliciano Bantilan earned his AB Philosophy from St Francis Xavier Major Seminary, Davao City, Philippines. After his MS Physics from University of the Philippines at Diliman, Quezon City, he went to the USA on fellowship to pursue a PhD in Physics. He obtained his PhD in Physics from Duke University in 1983. He returned to his country and taught Physics at the University of the Philippines at Los Banos.

Then, a bombshell dropped on his life: Parkinson's disease in 2002. The lowest point in his struggle with Parkinson's occurred in 2006, when his mobility was so impaired, he no longer could raise himself up on bed to sleep. He slept on a mattress spread on the floor. He would have episodes of near panic, due to difficulty breathing. Then, by a stroke of luck, still with severe movement difficulty--only a finger in his left hand could press keys of his laptop--he chanced upon the website of Dr Amy Yasko.

A year and three months into her protocol, he began to get back some of his mobility, as well as some of his "brain". And something more: all of a sudden, he began to think in verse. He enjoyed reading and reciting poetry since he was young. However, he never composed a poem in his life, until his partial recovery. At age sixty-five, he began writing poetry. The first two poems he composed make up his first book published in 2013, *Einstein in Verse: Introduction to Special and General*

Relativity. The rest forms the content of his second book published in 2014, *Life in Poetry: The Evolutionary 'Garden of Eden'*. This is his third book, *IQ plus EQ: The Arrow and the Hoisting Crane.*

Other books by the author

Einstein in Verse: Introduction to Special and General Relativity

Life in Poetry: The Evolutionary "Garden of Eden"